A SOUTHERN
GARDENER'S NOTEBOOK

William D. Adams

William C. Welch
TEXAS AND THE
GULF SOUTH

Don Hastings
MID-SOUTH

Stan DeFreitas
FLORIDA

TAYLOR PUBLISHING COMPANY
DALLAS, TEXAS

William C. Welch

ALSO BY WILLIAM C. WELCH:

Antique Roses for the South
Perennial Garden Color

ALSO BY DON HASTINGS:

Gardening in the South: Flowers, Vines, & Houseplants
Gardening in the South: Trees, Shrubs, & Lawns
Gardening in the South: Vegetables & Fruit

ALSO BY STAN DeFREITAS:

The Water-Thrifty Garden
The Complete Guide To Florida Gardening

Published by Taylor Publishing Company
          1550 West Mockingbird Lane
          Dallas, Texas 75235

Designed by Hespenheide Design

Printed in the United States of America

10 9 8 7 6 5 4 3 2 1

CONTENTS

Perennials for Southern Gardens   4

Planning Your Garden   7

The Dirt on Southern Soils   14

Hardiness Zone Map   17

Planting Charts

    Perennials   18

    Annuals   20

    Vegetables   21

January   23

February   35

March   47

    Growing Your Own Groceries   60

April   65

May   77

June   91

    Planting Fruit Trees   102

    Vertical Gardening   103

July   107

August   119

September   131

    Accessories for the Garden   143

October   147

November   159

December   171

Notes

    Plants   183

    Pests and Diseases   189

    Weather   190

    Soil Tests   191

Plant of the Month profiles by William C. Welch

PERENNIALS FOR SOUTHERN GARDENS

by Dr. William C. Welch

Perennials may be defined as plants that return year after year from the same root part. They are versatile plants that offer a variety of creative uses in the garden. From tiny terrace gardens of inner city apartments to extensive country estate gardens, perennials often add color, form, and texture for many years and require minimum maintenance. A look at some of the landscape possibilities should help stimulate ideas for specific additions to your own garden.

THE PERENNIAL BORDER

We inherited the perennial border style, as we know it today, from England. It is a version of the cottage gardens that evolved during the seventeenth and eighteenth centuries. The two greatest popularizers of this planting style were Gertrude Jekyll (1843-1932) and William Robinson (1838-1935), who proposed it as a rebellion against Victorian gardens, landscapes that Robinson once described as "the ugliest gardens ever made." Typically, the gardens of upper class Victorians featured rigid, geometric masses of brightly colored annuals, all maintained at a uniform height like tufts in a carpet. This style was known as "bedding out," and it had gained popularity after 1845 when the British government lifted the

tax on glass. By lowering the cost of building materials for greenhouses on residential estates, the measure made it possible to produce annuals economically and in quantity.

In place of these monotonous floral carpets, Jekyll and Robinson beautifully articulated more natural combinations of plants, primarily perennials, both in the gardens they designed and through their writings. They extended the flower season from a few months in spring and summer to all year long with the use of bulbs, ornamental grasses, and old-fashioned plants and herbs collected from the simple gardens of English cottagers. Earth and plant forms inspired the new concept of garden design as the plants' season, ecology, and arrangement in nature created the basis for the design revolution so clearly espoused by these two pioneers.

Jekyll was an accomplished painter until her eyesight began to fail when she was in her forties, at which point she began fully devoting her talents to the garden. Taking the earth as her canvas and plants as her palette, she went to work on what she considered the ultimate expression of garden art—the herbaceous border. Jekyll fashioned beautiful pictures by carefully selecting plants and then arranging them in the long clumps of color she referred to as "drifts."

Through her selection of plants, Jekyll also varied forms, heights, color, and textures within her borders. To be successful, she believed, the designer must ultimately know the growing habits and requirements as well as aesthetic qualities of the plants.

English herbaceous borders were almost always limited in space by constructed walls or hedges. These walls or hedges not only physically limited the garden space, but also provided a sense of continuity and organization to the composition. Strong, simple organization contrasts with the wide variety of plants, with each plant displaying distinct colors, forms, and textures and reaching its peak at a different time of the year.

THE SOUTHERN PERSPECTIVE

Our growing conditions in the South require that plants overcome a combination of very high temperatures and generally high humidity. Our summers don't just fry vegetation, they steam and broil it overnight. Not only must a plant survive under these conditions, it must also bloom, grow well under minimal care, and make a good display in the garden. Among the perennials, the majority of plants that fulfill these criteria are natives, native hybrids, or very special imports.

Choosing the right cultivars becomes essential to success, but a problem may be finding commercial sources for the plants. There is a very welcome movement afoot in the southern nursery trade to satisfy the public demand for more adapted perennials and now good choices are available.

Because division is necessary for many perennials, quite often the more rare plants are obtained from friends and neighbors who share their "extras." Excellent cultivars are often obtained by

swapping with experienced local gardeners, and through market bulletins and magazines. When in bloom, the wild plant should be clearly and permanently marked, the seed gathered and sown soon afterward for most perennials. This way you know what the plant will look like and can preserve it in the garden while conserving the wild population.

The catchword in the drier parts of the South and Southwest is "Xeriscape," a concept that promotes the use of plants and landscape design practices that require little irrigation water. With the increasing need to conserve our water resources, this is a relevant concept indeed. Fortunately, there are many plants that require little more water, if any more at all, than nature provides for our southern gardens.

THE COTTAGE GARDEN

Southern cottage gardens have always held a special fascination. Often the product of very limited resources, these plantings teach valuable lessons in garden lay-out, plant choice, and cultivation methods—all tried and true over years of hardship, climatic and otherwise. The classic cottage garden was typically an enclosed front-door yard, surrounded by picket fencing or hedges. A straight walk usually led from a rose-covered arch at the entry gate to the porch and front door. Sometimes stone, brick, or dirt paths also led from the main entrance around the house. The total area was quite small, but there was rarely turf within the enclosed garden. Instead, there was an interesting mixture of roses, perennials, reseeding annuals, herbs, and occasional fruit trees and small flowering trees such as redbud, dogwood, or crape myrtle. No two cottage gardens were ever just alike, but the style is easily recognized.

The plants were likely to have been handed down within families or shared as treasure among friends and neighbors. This concept of garden design is becoming more popular again today as homeowners seek ways to include a diverse population of plants and still have a strong design theme. Townhouses, apartment dwellings, and zero-lot-line housing are good candidates for cottage gardens.

Cottage gardens and perennial borders are certainly not the only ways to utilize perennials in our gardens. Other possibilities include containers; woodland, cutflower, color theme and water gardens; mixed borders; and color pockets in existing landscapes.

Southerners need not feel apologetic about all the perennials they can grow well. The list differs radically from those grown in the colder parts of the nation, but our palette is large and interesting. By exploring southern gardening heritage and carefully examining new plants and techniques, today's southern gardener can create a distinctive and exciting landscape featuring colorful perennials in bloom at any time of the year.

William C. Welch

PLANNING YOUR GARDEN

by Stan DeFreitas

Most everyone can pick out landscapes that are poorly designed. These are the landscapes that have a "hit-or-miss" look, where it's apparent that the plantings were set independently of a concept or plan. To get the most enjoyment out of your yard, and consequently your home, it's important to create a landscape design for your plot. Making a plan and following it enables you to use your land the most efficiently.

A landscape design is developed by dividing your yard into three main areas: the public area, the private area, and the service area. The public area includes the parts of your yard, and the elements they contain, that create a "setting" for your home, usually your front yard and/or lawn. The private area may be used for entertaining guests and as a place for leisure activities. The service area is designated for practical uses, such as tool storage and work space.

Develop the **public area** around existing trees. Your goal should be to end up with enough trees in the front lawn area to create a nice frame for your home. Remember to consider a tree's mature size and shape before incorporating it into the design. Small flowering trees, such as the bottlebrush, can grow to 10 feet tall, while large sycamores can grow to 70 feet tall. Some trees, like Italian cypresses, have a narrow shape and others, like live oaks, might cover the entire front lawn

area. These all work nicely within landscapes—as long as the design allows for their eventual sizes and shapes.

There are several basic plantings that are commonly used to soften the look of a plot and complement a home. Many people plant large trees alongside their homes to shield the structure, and to also cool and provide shade in the summer, without eliminating or vastly reducing the view. Flowering trees serve as focal points and are good additions to any landscape. Foundation plantings, often shrubs such as *Viburnums* or hollies (coarsely textured plants), conceal the bases of homes. Fine-textured plants, such as ferns, cuphea, or other small-leafed plants, work well along entryways. Fragrant plants like roses, gardenias, and jasmines are also good choices to line entryways.

When planning your landscape, you have the option of planting everything at one time or doing it gradually. Trees can be added over a number of growing seasons, and perennial plant borders and annuals can also be added at the same time. Remember that a well-thought-out plan, even a simple one, will have a lasting effect on your landscape. Planning for permanent fixtures, such as trees and shrubs in your plot will save you time and money in the long run.

The **private area** can also be considered the outdoor living area. Quite often this area is in the back of the home. The space here is sometimes limited, but can be combined with either of the other areas (public or service). Living in a fast-paced world makes many of us more interested in having privacy around our homes. The outdoor living area is a perfect answer to this need. It's the perfect area for outdoor entertaining. This may also be the part of your yard that best accommodates a garden or a child's sandbox. Private areas can be designed to give different degrees of privacy—you just have to decide what's right for your family's needs.

On large lots, a mass of evergreen trees can be used as a natural screen to enclose the private area. In smaller lots, a wooden fence or wall is a great choice and accomplishes the same thing as a wall of trees. Grouping tall container plants also works well to define different areas. Most designs can be arranged with lots of plantings in mind, but remember to select both quality and quantity when choosing plants for any area. You might use popular thorny-type plants, such as hollies, boxthorns, and roses, to define an area, but remember they can also present problems if planted along traffic patterns.

Areas that are considered work spaces or **service areas** are necessities. This is where the garbarge cans, mowers, sheds (for garden tool storage), and other outdoor equipment is stored. With the proper placement of plants, these service areas can be softened with the use of trellises, vines, and larger plantings (small shrubs or trees).

THE DESIGN

Once you've determined your family's needs, you're ready to plan the design. One of the first steps in planning a landscape design is to roughly determine the plot's grade and drainage patterns. The water should run off the property, or to a specific site on the property. Stake out any changes that may be necessary to allow proper drainage.

Also use stakes to measure out areas where walkways, driveways, and certain garden areas will be. Learn where water, electric, and telephone lines are and flag these areas as well. If you are not sure exactly where these lines lie, check with the local utility companies to confirm their locations. This way you will know where to dig with caution when putting in an irrigation system or the plant material selected for those sites. This is an **essential** step before you undertake any construction.

As with any design, too many different types of plants (what designers refer to as the Noah's Arc effect—a little bit of everything) will make for a poorly organized landscape. Create your design with simplicity in mind. Make sure all plants you choose have a basic function in the landscape. Before you add a plant to the landscape, position it where you intend to plant it and check to see whether the effect is the one you expected. Another general guideline is to choose plant material (ground covers, vining plants, and shrubs or trees) that are well proportioned to the area in which they will be planted. The "Plant of the Month" selections and the "What to Plant" tips that follow will hopefully spark your creativity.

Planting a large tree in a small lot is a common mistake. Although a large tree provides shade and is visually pleasing, it often overshadows a home, making it appear much smaller. And large trees cause other problems too. For example, a *Ficus benjamina* planted in a small lot will literally lift up a sidewalk or driveway. Oaks are also misplanted in this manner. Despite their popularity, these trees are simply too large for smaller plots. Be practical when making plant material choices and base your selections on your landscape's needs and limitations. Your local nursery or extension office can help answer questions about potential plant problems.

When creating a design it's usually more helpful to sketch out a plan first. Begin by making a list of what you want to keep in your yard and what you want to move. Next, make a list of your favorite plants, or those you want to incorporate into the design. On graph paper (see the following pages) experi-ment by drawing up various plans, being careful to note the location of your home; driveway; sidewalks; existing trees, shrubs, and plants you want to keep; utility lines; and traffic patterns.

As you work on your plan, remember that repetition and flowing lines are good design guidelines to follow because they are easy on the eye. Also consider that corner plants help soften building lines and that most landscapes benefit from having flowering trees, hardy plants, and, in the coastal South, tropicals.

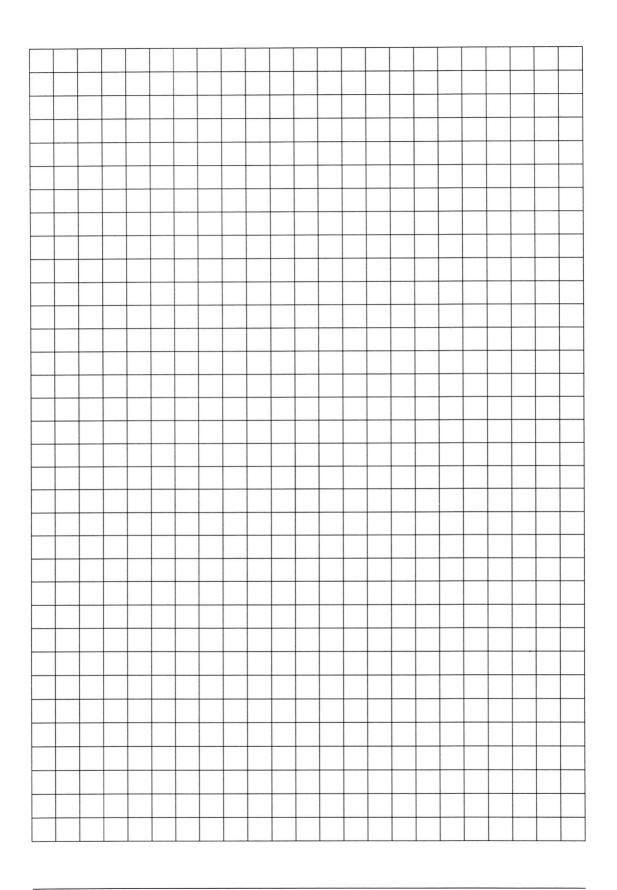

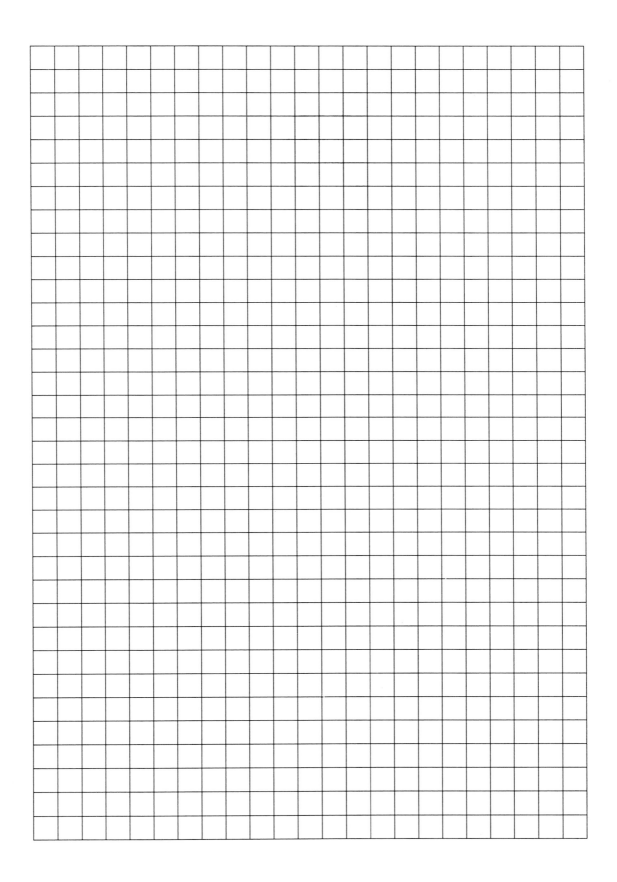

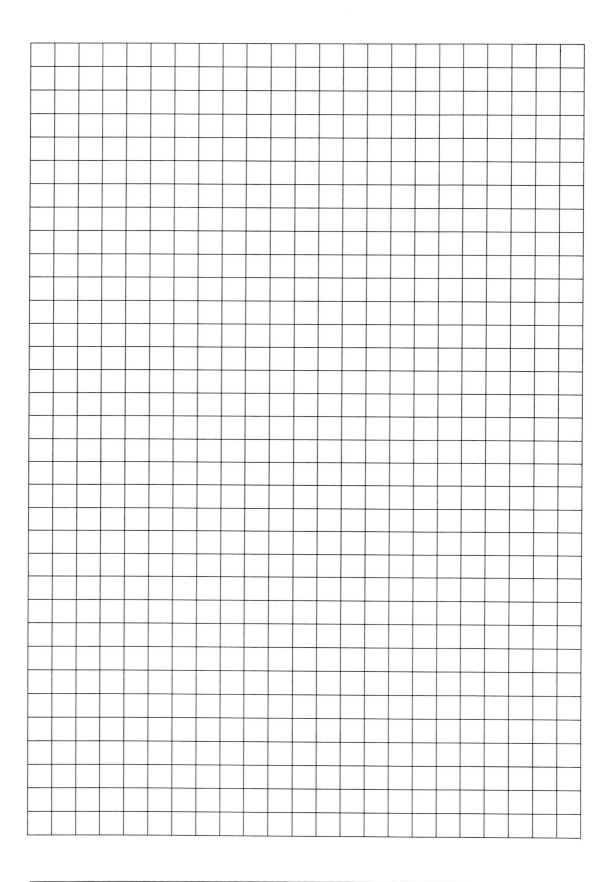

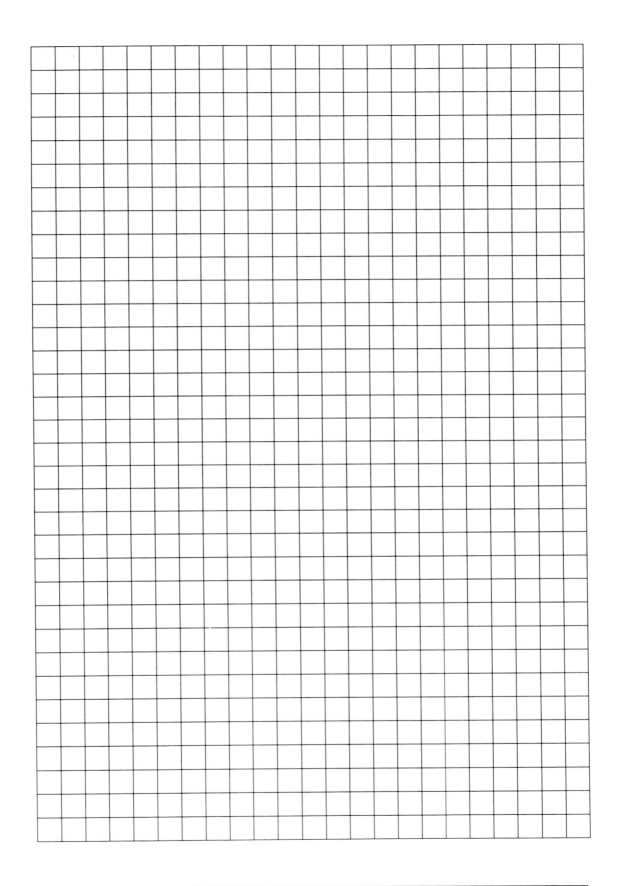

THE DIRT ON SOUTHERN SOILS

by Don Hastings

There is nothing wrong with southern soils. In the late 1700s, Englishman William Bartram traveled through much of the South and described the amazing fertility of its soils. It is what has happened to them over the ages since Europeans came to this part of the United States that's the problem. The Native American farmers had done well with the land, putting back into the soil as much as their crops took out, but years of later farming abuse and today's bulldozers have destroyed or reduced the fertility of much of the land. Clay soils of the South have been the most depleted, while mountains and the coastal plain soils remain more fertile. However, gardeners in every part of the South must constantly work to improve the fertility of the soils in which they plant.

It is not a difficult task but it is a constant one. The long growing season and high summer temperatures increase the bacterial activity in the ground, which causes the breakdown and disappearance of organic matter. Organic matter is essential for good soil structure as well as fertility. Without it, clay soil becomes sticky and slick when wet, and hard as a brick when dry. Without humus, sandy loam soil lacks fertility and water-holding capacity.

Successful gardening starts with a soil-building and maintenance program. Yearly incorporation of organic matter is the first step and there are several ways to do it:

Compost

Every gardener has a potential for vast amounts of excellent organic matter from tree leaves and dead herbaceous plant material in the fall. Both are available in great quantities and should be made into compost rather than thrown away.

A compost area is an indispensable part of a successful garden. Leaves and herbaceous plant material that are composted in the fall are ready to be worked into the ground the following spring. The yearly addition of compost is vital to the fertility of the soil.

Peat Moss

Sphagnum peat moss is a commercially available material that is an excellent source of organic matter. It usually comes in bales. It is ready to incorporate into the ground at any time needed.

Ground Bark

Finely ground pine bark is an effective, long-lasting source of organic matter. It is particularly good as an amendment to improve the drainage and structure of the soil.

Green Manure

Growing humus is another way to increase the organic matter in soils. Green manure crops produce large amounts of succulent material that may then be plowed into the ground ahead of planting. They decompose rapidly. Green manure crops are also excellent for garden areas that will remain bare all winter to prevent erosion during heavy winter rains.

The South is particularly fortunate in having good green manure crops that may be planted in the late summer or fall, grown during the winter, and are ready to plow in before the spring crops.

Crimson clover can be planted in September and October after summer flowers and vegetables have finished. It will be ready to turn under in March.

Austrian winter pea is an excellent green manure crop that germinates in colder soil than crimson clover. Plant it in late October and November after fall flowers and vegetables have been killed by frost. It will be ready for turning under in April.

Both of these plants are legumes, which add nitrogen to the soil while growing. There are many other green manure crops, such as annual ryegrass, common rye, and even weeds. However in the South, crimson clover and Austrian winter pea are the best.

Commercial Additives

There is a growing awareness of the role of organics in the vitality of soils. Much research has been done on a group of materials called lignites, which are mined in parts of the United States and are commercially available to gardeners. These materials can improve soils tremendously—especially when planting lawns, for which yearly additions of organic matter are impossible.

* * *

Growing good plants starts with keeping the organic material in southern soils, but does not end there. The nutrient levels are generally low, and additional amounts must be given on a regular basis in the form of fertilizer. Adding humus on a regular basis allows gardeners to use chemical fertilizers for the source of nutrients. These are more potent and are less expensive for the amount of nutrients obtained than organic fertilizers. However, soils deficient in organic matter are helped by the addition of organic fertilizers such as blood meal, chicken manure, cow manure, cottonseed meal, and fish meal in addition to chemical fertilizers.

The important factor in fertilizing properly is the amount of each nutrient in the source material. Organic fertilizers with very low nutrient levels act more as soil builders than as fertilizers. Plants may perform better than without any additional organics, but certainly poorer than when the soil has good organic content *and* the right amounts of nutrients from chemical fertilizers.

The pH of the soil also may determine success or failure. This measure of the acidity or alkalinity of the soil guides the gardener in determining what to plant in a spot or whether a correction needs to be made. On a scale of 0 to 24, low numbers indicate acidity while numbers above 7 (neutral) show alkalinity. For example, most broadleaf evergreens need to grow in soil with a rather low pH of 5 to 5.5. Herbaceous vegetables and flowers generally grow best in a soil with a pH around 6.5 to 7. Add ground limestone to raise the pH of soil or aluminum sulphate to lower it. Some organic materials, like peat moss and cottonseed meal, help to lower the pH amd are excellent to use in planting evergreens or other types of plants that need acid soil as well as humus.

Good gardening practices are also extremely important for success. Organic matter placed on top of the soil has little chance of helping plants, whose roots are deep in the ground. Fertilizer scattered around plants that are growing in brick-like soil can never adequately reach roots and benefit plants. Good gardening in the South requires a total program that starts with soil preparation and ends when the growing season is over.

Soil Preparation

Organic matter must be incorporated into the entire root zone of the plants or it will accomplish little. Good soil preparation begins with some method of breaking up the soil as deep as the roots will penetrate. This allows the organic matter as well as limestone to be mixed with the area where the plant will grow. The easiest way to work large areas is with a rotary tiller whose tines cut into the soil, break it up and pulverize it.

Till an area thoroughly until the tines are cutting deeply as is possible with the type machine. Apply organic material and limestone, if needed. Till again to incorporate these materials into the entire root zone.

Tree and shrub planting may be done with a shovel. Dig a large, deep hole. Thoroughly incorporate the organic matter into the soil removed from the hole. Then plant according to instructions.

When to Plow

Should gardens be plowed when the soil is moist and soft or when it is dry and hard? Clay soils can be made unmanage-able when plowed or worked too wet, for doing so destroys the structure of the soil. It is always better to work soil when it is dry. Of course, this presents a problem, as much soil preparation is done in the spring when there is the most rain.

Since many plants need to be set out on a strict schedule, timing, then, is important. Plan ahead. Decide where gardens will be so that the soil may be prepared before the last minute. Work the soil well ahead of planting time whenever it is not too wet.

There is a simple test to determine whether the soil is too wet to work. Scratch up a handful of earth and squeeze it tightly into a ball in your palm. Release your fingers and try to break up the ball with your thumb. If the ball breaks into small crumbles, it is a good time to work the soil. If the ball breaks into large clumps and is sticky, it is too wet.

Keeping Soil Loose After Planting

After heavy rains, southern clay and clay-loam soils tend to develop a surface crust that prevents air, water, and fertilizer from penetrating the soil. Poor growth results. Farmers cultivate their crops frequently to break this crust and gardeners should do the same. A three-pronged cultivator or pointed hoe is an excellent tool for this task. Tillers may also be used for cultivating plants, but rows must be far apart enough to prevent the tines from damaging roots.

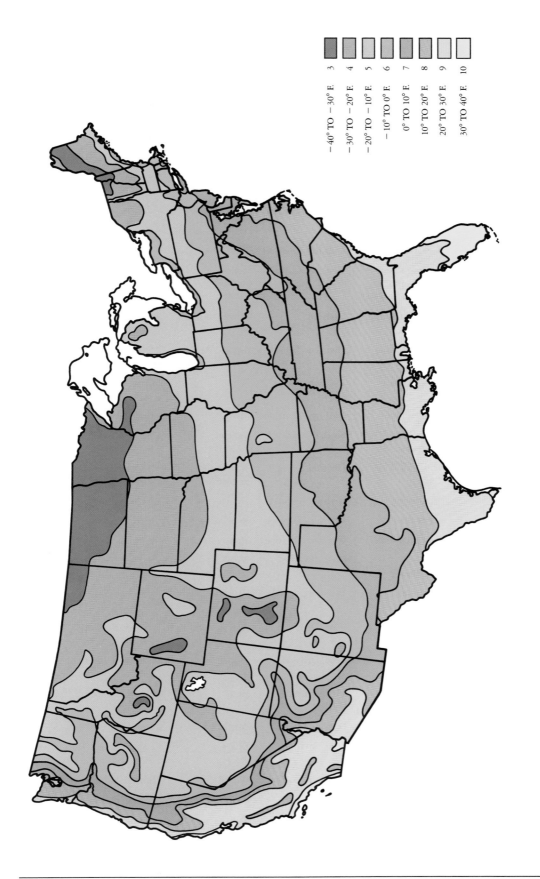

APPROXIMATE RANGE OF AVERAGE ANNUAL MINIMUM TEMPERATURES

−40° TO −30° F.	3
−30° TO −20° F.	4
−20° TO −10° F.	5
−10° TO 0° F.	6
0° TO 10° F.	7
10° TO 20° F.	8
20° TO 30° F.	9
30° TO 40° F.	10

PARTIAL LIST OF PERENNIALS FOR SOUTHERN LANDSCAPES

Botanical Name	Common Name	Propagation	Flower Color	Flowering Season	Height
Achillea sp.	Yarrow	Seed, Division	White, Rose, Yellow	Summer	1'
Allium sp.	Garlic, Chives	Division	White	Summer	1'
Aquilegia chrysantha "Hinckleyana"	Hinckley's Columbine	Seed, Division	Yellow	Spring	18"
Aquilegia canadensis	Columbine	Seed, Division	Yellow/Red Blend	Spring	2'
Artemisia 'Powis Castle'	Artemisia	Cuttings, Division	Gray foliage	—	2'–3'
Asclepias tuberosa	Butterfly Weed	Seed	Yellow/Red	Summer	2'
Aster oblongifolius	Fall Aster	Cuttings, Division	Lavender	Fall	3'
Beloperone guttata	Shrimp Plant (Gold and Red-brown selections)	Division, Cuttings	Yellow or Red-brown	Summer, Fall	3'
Bletilla striata	Chinese Ground Orchid	Division	Purple, White	Spring	1'–2'
Canna x *generalis*	Garden Canna	Division, Tubers	Yellow, Red, Pink, Salmon	Summer	2'–4'
Chrysanthemum leucanthemum	Ox-eye Daisy	Division, Seed	White	Spring	3'
Chrysanthemum sp.	Garden Mums	Cuttings, Division	Many	Fall	3'
Coreopsis grandiflora	Baby Sun Coreopsis	Seed, Division	Yellow	Late Spring, Summer	1'
Crinum sp.	Milk and Wine Lily	Division	White, rose, pink, and striped	Spring, Summer, Fall	2'–4'
Crocosmia pottsii	Montbretia	Division (corms)	Orange-red	Early Summer	2'–3'
Cuphea micropetala	Cigar Plant	Cuttings, Division	Red/Yellow	Summer, Fall	3'–4'
Dianthus sp.	Perennial Pink	Cuttings, Division	Many	Spring	1'
Echinacea angustifolia	Purple Coneflower	Seed, Division	Purple	Spring, Summer, Fall	18"
Eupatorium coelestinum	Perennial Ageratum	Division	Lavender-blue	Summer, Fall	3'
Gaillardia sp.	Indian Blanket	Seed, Division	Red-yellow blend	Spring, Summer, Fall	18"
Gaura lindheimeri	Gaura	Seed, Division	White	Spring, Summer, Fall	2'
Gerbera sp.	Gerbera Daisy (Transvaal)	Tissue Culture, Seed	Many	Spring, Summer, Fall	2'
Gladiolus byzantinus	Corn Flag	Division (corms)	Purple, white	Summer	3'
Helianthus maximiliani	Maximilian Sunflower	Seed, Division	Yellow	Late Summer, Fall	3'–4'
Hemerocallis	Day Lily	Division	Many	Spring, Summer	1'–3'
Hosta sp.	Plaintain Lily	Division	White	Spring, Summer	1'–3'
Ipheion uniflorum	Spring Star Flower	Division	Blue	Spring	6"

Botanical Name	Common Name	Propagation	Flower Color	Flowering Season	Height
Iris, Bearded	Bearded Iris	Division	Many	Spring	1'–3'
Iris, Dutch	Dutch Iris	Division	Many	Spring	1'–3'
Iris, Louisiana	Louisiana Iris	Division, Seed	Many	Spring	3'
Lantana montevidensis	Trailing Lantana	Division, Seed, Cuttings	Many	Spring, Summer, Fall	1'–2'
Lycoris radiata	Red Spider Lily	Division	Coral-red, White, Yellow	Fall	1'
Lythrum salicaria	Purple Loosestrife	Seed, Division	Lavender-Pink	Spring, Summer, Fall	2'–3'
Malvaviscus drummondii	Turk's Cap	Seed, Cuttings	Red	Spring, Summer, Fall	1'
Mentha piperita	Peppermint	Cuttings, Division	—	—	1'
Narcissus sp.	Daffodils and Narcissus	Division	Yellow, White	Spring	1'
Oxalis crassipes	Oxalis	Division	Pink	Spring, Summer	8"–10"
Pavonia lasiopetala	Rock Rose	Cuttings, Seed	Pink	Spring, Summer, Fall	3'–4'
Penstemon cobaea	Wild Foxglove	Seed, Division	Lavender	Spring	2'
Phlox divaricata	Louisiana Phlox	Division, Cuttings	Purple	Spring	1'–2'
Phlox paniculata	Perennial Phlox	Cuttings, Division	Lavender, Pink, White	Summer	2'
Phlox pilosa	Prairie Phlox	Cuttings, Division	Lavender-Pink	Spring	1'–2'
Phlox subulata	Thrift, Moss Pink	Cuttings, Division	Pink	Spring	8"–10"
Physostegia virginiana	Obedient Plant	Division	Lavender, White	Summer	3'
Plumbago auriculata	Blue Plumbago	Seed, Division	Blue, White	Summer, Fall	3'
Rhodophiala bifida	Oxblood Lily	Division	Dark Red	Fall	1'
Rosmarinus officinalis	Rosemary	Cuttings, Division	Blue	Summer, Fall	1'–4'
Salvia farinacea	Mealy Cup Sage	Seed, Division	Blue, White, Purple	Spring, Summer, Fall	3'
Salvia Greggii	Autumn Salvia	Cuttings, Seed	White, Red, Pink	Spring, Summer, Fall	2'–3'
Symphytum officinale	Comfrey	Division	White, Yellowish, Purple, Rose	Summer	3'
Tagetes lucida	Mexican Marigold-Mint	Cuttings, Division	Yellow	Summer, Fall	2'
Thymus vulgaris	Common Thyme	Division, Cuttings	—	—	6"
Verbena hybrida	Verbena	Seed, Division	Many	Spring, Summer, Fall	6"–1'
Viola odorata	Sweet Violet	Division	Purple	Winter, Spring	6"–8"
Zephyranthes candida	White Rain Lily	Division	White	Summer	1'
Zephyranthes grandiflora	Pink Rain Lily	Division	Pink	Summer	1'

ANNUALS PLANTING GUIDE

Botanical Name	Common Name	Flower Color	Planting Season*	Days To Bloom (Seeds)	Height
Ageratum spp.	Ageratum	blue, white, lavender	Feb.-April(F) March	75–80	6"–12"
Alcea rosea	Hollyhock	pink, red, white, varies	Aug.-Jan.(F) March	150–175	3'–5'
Antirrhinum majus	Snap dragon	yellow, pink, white, varies	Sept.-Dec.(F) March	90–120	6"–36"
Begonia spp.	Begonia	red, white, coral	All year (F) Jan.(T) March	75–90	6"–12"
Calendula officinalis	Calendula	yellow, orange	March	—	1'–2'
Celosia spp.	Cockscomb	red, gold, pink, varies	Feb.-April(F) March	60–80	2'
Cosmos spp.	Cosmos	orange, pink, yellow	Feb.-April(F) March	75	2'–4'
Dahlia spp.	Dahlia	red, white, varies	Feb.-March(F) March	50–60	3'–5'
Dianthus chinensis	Pinks	pink, red, white, combos	Sept.-Dec.(F) March	60–75	1'–2'
Eschscholzia californica	California Poppy	orange	Nov.-Jan.(F) March Feb.(T)	80–90	1'–2'
Gaillardia pulchella	Gaillardia	red, orange	Sept.-Jan.(F) March	60–75	18"–24"
Gerbera jamesonii	African Daisy	orange, red, yellow, pink	Aug.-Jan.(F) March	90	1'–2'
Gomphrena globusa	Globe Amaranth	fuchsia, some other colors	March-April(F) March	90	1'–3'
Helianthus annuus	Sunflower	yellow	March	—	5'–10'
Impatiens spp.	Impatiens	white, pink, coral, red	Feb.-July(F) March	65–90	1'–2'
Ipomoea purpurea	Morning Glory	blue, violet	Feb.-April(F) March	60–75	Vine
Lathyrus odoratus	Sweet Pea	pink, yellow, white, varies	Oct.-Jan.(F) Feb.-March	70–85	Vine
Lobularia maritima	Sweet Alyssum	white, violet, combos	Sept.-Jan.(F)	45	4"–6"
Mirabilis jalapa	Four O'clocks	purple, pink, white, multi	Feb.-May(F) March	60–75	18"–36"
Nicotiana alata	Flowering Tobacco	white, red, cream, more	Aug.-Nov.(F) March	90–100	1'–2½'
Pelargonium spp.	Geranium	red, magenta, pink, coral	Feb.-June(F) March	85–100	12"–24"
Petunia hybrida	Petunia	pink, purple, white, multi	Aug.-Jan.(F) Jan.(T)March	75–90	10"–20"
Phlox drummondii	Phlox	pink, white,	Aug.-Jan.(F) Feb.(T)	75	12"–24"
Portulaca grandiflora	Moss Rose	orange, red, yellow, pink, many more brights	Feb.-May(F) March	45–60	4"–8"
Senecio cineraria	Dusty Miller	silver foliage	March	—	1'–2'
Tagetes spp.	Marigold	orange, yellow	Feb.-May(F) March	45–60	8"–36"
Tropaeolum majus	Nasturtium	orange, red	Feb.-March(F) Feb.(T) March	60–80	8"–12"
Vinca rosea	Periwinkle, Vinca	violet, pink, white	Feb.(F) March	80–90	6"–24"
Viola wittrockiana	Pansy	purple, blue, yellow, multi	Sept.-Dec.(F)	90	6"–10"
Zinnia spp.	Zinnia	orange, pink	Feb.-Aug.(F) March	45–60	6"–36"

*(F) = Florida (T) = Texas

VEGETABLE PLANTING GUIDE

Name	Type	Edible Part	Way to Plant	When to Plant	When Ready	Length of Harvest
Artichoke, Jerusalem	Hardy Perennial	Tubers	Tubers	Winter	Fall	Many years
Asparagus	Hardy Perennial	Shoots	Start seeds	January	Summer 2nd year	Many years
Asparagus	Hardy Perennial	Shoots	2 yr. roots	Winter	First summer	Many years
Beans, Bush Lima	Tender Annual	Immature seed	Direct seeding	When ground warms	2½ months	Six weeks
Beans, Bush Snap	Tender Annual	Immature pods	Direct seeding	After frost	1½ to 2 months	One month
Beans, Pole Lima	Tender Annual	Immature seed	Direct seeding	After ground warms	Three months	Eight weeks
Beans, Pole Snap	Tender Annual	Immature pods	Direct seeding	After frost	2 to 3 months	6-8 weeks
Beet	Half-Hardy Annual	Roots	Direct seeding	After hard freezes	Two months	Two weeks
Broccoli	Hardy Annual	Immature flower head	*Plants	After hard freezes	Two months	Two weeks
Cabbage	Hardy Annual	Leaf head	*Plants	Spring after hard freezes	2-2½ months	Two weeks
Cabbage, Winter hardy types	Hardy Annual	Leaf head	*Plants	September	Early spring	Two weeks
Carrot	Half-Hardy Annual	Root	Direct seeding	After hard freezes	2½ months	One month
Cauliflower	Half-Hardy Annual	Immature flower head	*Plants	After hard freezes	Two months	Two weeks
Collard	Hardy Annual	Leaves	*Plants	After hard freezes	Two months	+-6 weeks
Collard, Fall	Hardy Annual	Leaves	*Plants	Late August	October and November	Two months
Corn, Sweet	Tender Annual	Immature seed (ears)	Direct seeding	After ground warms	Two to three months	Two weeks
Cowpea	Tender Annual	Immature seed	Direct seeding	After ground warms	Two to three months	Until frost
Cucumber	Tender Annual	Fruit	Direct seeding	After frost	Two months	Eight weeks
Eggplant	Tender Annual	Fruit	*Plants	After frost	Two months	All summer
Garlic	Hardy Annual	Bulb	Set cloves	Fall or spring	Three months	Two weeks
Lettuce, Heading type	Half-Hardy Annual	Leaf head	Seed or *Plants	After hard freezes	Three months	Two weeks
Lettuce, Leaf type	Half-Hardy Annual	Leaves	Seed or *Plants	After hard freezes	1½ months	Three to four weeks
Melon, Cantaloupe	Tender Annual	Fruit	Direct seeding	After ground warms	Two to three months	Two weeks
Melon, Honey Dew	Tender Annual	Fruit	Direct seeding	After ground warms	Three months	Two weeks
Mustard Green, Fall	Half-Hardy Annual	Leaves	Direct seeding	Late August/September	One month	Until hard freezes
Mustard Green, Spring	Half-Hardy Annual	Leaves	Direct seeding	After hard freezes	1½ months	Two months
Okra	Tender Annual	Immature pods	Direct seeding	After ground warms	Two months	Ten weeks
Onion, Plants	Hardy Annual	Bulbs	Plants	Fall or late winter	Three months	Two weeks
Onion, Sets	Hardy Annual	Green leaves	Sets	Fall or late winter	One month	Until hot weather
Peas, English Smooth Seeded	Half-Hardy Annual	Immature seed	Direct seeding	Winter	Three months	Until hot weather
Peas, Snap type	Half-Hardy Annual	Immature pods	Direct seeding	After hard freezes	Two months	Until hot weather
Peas, Snow Type	Hardy Annual	Pods	Direct seeding	Winter	Two months	Until hot weather
Pepper, Sweet and Hot	Tender annual	Immature fruit	*Plants	After ground warms	2½ months	Until fall frost
Potato, Irish	Hardy Annual	Tuber	Parts of tubers	Late winter	Three to four months	Two weeks
Potato, Sweet	Tender Annual	Root	**Plants	After ground warms	Fall	Until frost
Pumpkin	Tender Annual	Fruit	Direct seeding	After ground warms	3 to 4 months	Two weeks
Radish, Spring	Half-Hardy Annual	Root	Direct seeding	After freezes	One month	Until hot weather
Shallot	Hardy Annual	Bulbs	Bulbs	August-September	June	One month
Spinach	Half-Hardy Annual	Leaves	Direct seeding	After freezes	1½ months	Until hot weather
Squash, Summer	Tender Annual	Fruit	Direct seeding	After ground warms	Two months	Eight weeks
Squash, Winter	Tender Annual	Fruit	Direct seeding	After ground warms	Two to three months	3 weeks
Squash, Zucchini	Tender Annual	Fruit	Direct seeding	After ground warms	Two months	Eight weeks
Swiss Chard	Half-Hardy Annual	Leaves	Direct seeding	After frost	Two months	Until fall freezes
Tomato	Tender Annual	Fruit	*Plants	After frost	Two to three months	Until fall frost
Turnip, Fall Greens	Half-Hardy Annual	Leaves	Direct seeding	August-September	1½ months	Until hard freezes
Turnip, Fall Roots	Half-Hardy Annual	Roots	Direct seeding	August	Late October/November	Until hard freezes
Turnip, Spring Greens	Half-Hardy Annual	Leaves	Direct seeding	After hard freezes	One month	Until hot weather
Turnip, Spring Roots	Half-Hardy Annual	Root	Direct seeding	After hard freezes	Two months	Until hot weather
Watermelon	Tender Annual	Fruit	Direct seeding	After ground warms	Three months	Two weeks

*SEEDS MAY BE SOWN IN TRAYS SIX WEEKS AHEAD OF PLANTING   **SWEET POTATO PLANTS (SLIPS) SHOULD BE PURCHASED

JANUARY

WHAT TO PLANT

Mid-South

Gardens in the mid-South never sleep. Even during the dead of winter there is much to do during breaks in the weather when temperatures are relatively mild. January is a variable month. The early part is often warm and balmy and a perfect time to start the year's first plantings in vegetable and flower gardens. The later part may be cold and miserable and is a good time to start seeds inside. Shrubs, trees, roses, and fruits may be planted whenever the ground is not frozen.

Plantings that can be started outside include: asparagus roots, horseradish roots, rhubarb roots, Jerusalem artichoke roots, hardy English pea seed, garlic cloves, onion sets for green onions, onion plants for large bulbs, hardy perennial roots, hardy biennial roots, sweet pea seed, peonies, bearded iris, dormant fruit and nut trees (potted, balled, or bare-root), dormant fruiting vines (potted or bare-root), and dormant bush fruits (potted, balled, or bare-root).

Start seeds for the following vegetables and flowers inside: asparagus, broccoli, cabbage, cauliflower, collards, Black-seeded Simpson lettuce, heading lettuce, parsley, hardy herbs, hardy annuals, hardy biennials, and hardy perennials.

Texas and the Gulf South

January is an excellent time to plant trees (including fruit trees) and shrubs. This is also the time to plant roses. If you're waiting for mail order bare-root roses, prepare the beds or individual holes as weather permits. This allows the mixture of organic material, fertilizer, and existing soil to weather till your roses arrive. Redigging the holes is easy when the major preparation is done ahead of time. Petunias and begonias should be sown in early January. Sow seeds inside in flats or containers to generate plant growth before the hot weather comes. Warm temperature plants such as tomatoes, peppers, marigolds, and periwinkles should be sown later in the month.

Florida

Arbor Day is usually in April, but in Florida it's unofficially designated as the third Friday in January. This is one of the best times of the year to plant shade trees. Some choices for planting might be: a live oak, camphor, laurel oak, water oak, sweetgum, red maple, American holly, East Palatka holly, southern magnolia, or Indian rosewood.

FEEDING

Mid-South

Fertilize all trees, including fruit trees, but do not feed figs. Wait until pruning time to fertilize roses and evergreen shrubs.

Jerry Pavia

Texas and the Gulf South

Apply small amounts of fertilizer on established pansy plantings. Use $1/2$ pound ammonium sulfate per 100 square feet of bed area. Repeat the application every 4 to 6 weeks, depending on rainfall. Dried blood meal is also an excellent source of fertilizer for pansies, calendulas, stock poppies, larkspur, and other cool-season annuals.

Florida

Now is the time to fertilize the Bermuda grass or ryegrass you planted this season. If you have not planted ryegrass, you still can at a rate of about 5 to 15 pounds per 1000 square feet.

GARDEN TASKS

Mid-South

Spray fruit trees with dormant spray. Use lime sulphur on peaches, plums, apricots, nectarines, and cherries. Use a dormant oil on apples and pears. Spray roses with lime sulphur. Prune shade trees for shaping. (Never prune the main leader because that would ruin the tree's shape.)

Texas and the Gulf South

Begin rose pruning in coastal areas. Remember that climbers and other once-blooming roses are best pruned after their spring flowers have faded. Select and order gladiolus corms for February and March planting. Allow for 2-week planting intervals to prolong the flowering period. Prepare planting areas for spring as weather allows.

Florida

Apply the first spray of the year on citrus. Trees that have been infected with brown rot, scab, or other common fungus can benefit from an application of neutral copper, sometimes sold as liquid copper. At this time, many people add an insecticide, such as Malathion. This will help reduce aphids, whiteflies, scales, and mites. As always, read and follow label directions and be safe!

Roses need to be trimmed back during the dormant season. Because this is normally the coldest month of the year, it's a good time to do it. This should be the most severe trimming of the year. Trim back about one-third to one-half of the rose's growth. Through trimming, you can also get rid of some of the dieback and black spot that often afflicts roses.

TROUBLESHOOTING

Mid-South

Watch for scale on evergreens. Spray with Cygon or Orthene for effective control.

Texas and the Gulf South

Check junipers and other narrowleaf evergreens for bagworm pouches (they look like pointed bags). The insect eggs overwinter in the pouches and start the cycle again by emerging in spring to feed on new foliage. Remove the pouches and destroy them to reduce the potential damage next spring.

Florida

Start watching mango and avocado trees for blooms that may appear this month. They are not too spectacular on these trees, but the fruit is worth the watch. A disease called anthracnose will appear first as small black, sunken areas on the flower spikes of mangoes and on the flowers and fruit of avocados. To prevent the disease, begin spray treatment with neutral copper when the blooms first appear and continue spraying weekly until the fruit is fully formed. After that, spray monthly until June.

FIRST
PART
OF THE
MONTH

_____

_____

_____

_____

_____

_____

_____

_____

_____

_____

_____

_____

_____

_____

_____

_____

_____

_____

_____

_____

_____

_____

SPECIAL TIPS

To start seeds inside, choose a brightly lighted place with mild temperatures during the daytime and cool temperatures at night. Sow seeds in a seed tray filled with a peat-light soil mixture. Cover the tray with a plastic sheet until the seeds have sprouted.

Extend the life of potted flowering plants received as Christmas gifts by keeping their soil moist and providing drainage so that the excess moisture can flow from their pots. Also keep plants out of heating ducts' direct airflow range— most potted flowering plants prefer cool temperatures between 60° and 65°F.

DON'T FORGET TO PUT
OUT BIRD FEEDERS
FOR OUR FEATHERED
FRIENDS WHO FLY
SOUTH FOR THE WINTER.
YOU WILL GET HOURS
OF ENJOYMENT FROM
WATCHING RED BIRDS
AND OTHER SPECIES
FEEDING.

Florida

IF YOU ARE GROWING
PEACHES, APPLES,
PEARS, PERSIMMONS,
OR GRAPES, PRUNE
THEM BACK NOW. THIS
WILL ALLOW LIGHT TO
ENTER THE CENTER OF
THE PLANT TO PRODUCE
BETTER GROWTH AND
FRUITING NEXT SEASON.

_____

_____

_____

_____

_____

_____

_____

_____

_____

_____

_____

_____

_____

_____

_____

_____

_____

_____

_____

_____

_____

_____

_____

SECOND PART OF THE MONTH

SPECIAL TIPS

KEEP HOUSEPLANTS ON A MAINTENANCE FERTILIZING SCHEDULE. DO NOT OVERWATER.

UTILIZE BAD WEATHER TO PLAN FLOWER AND VEGETABLE GARDENS. TIME SPENT ON ARMCHAIR GARDENING BEFORE THE FIREPLACE WILL PAY OFF IN THE SPRING WHEN THE PLANTING RUSH BEGINS.

Florida

JANUARY IS OUR COOLEST MONTH AND THE BEST TIME TO TRANSPLANT TREES AND WOODY ORNAMENTALS. BY PLANTING OR TRANS-PLANTING NOW, YOU WILL LESSEN THE SHOCK TO THE PLANT CAUSED BY THE PROCEDURE. REMEMBER, THERE IS A DEFINITE RELATIONSHIP BETWEEN A TREE'S TOP AND ITS ROOT SYSTEM. IF YOU LOSE A THIRD OF THE ROOT SYSTEM, CUT THE SAME AMOUNT OFF THE TOP. WHEN YOU MAKE THE NEW HOLE, DIG IT TWICE AS WIDE AND TWICE AS DEEP AS THE ROOT BALL. ADD PEAT MOSS AND DEHY-DRATED COW MANURE TO THE EXISTING SOIL IN THE PLANTING HOLE.

THIRD PART OF THE MONTH

_____

_____

_____

_____

_____

_____

_____

_____

_____

_____

_____

_____

_____

_____

_____

_____

_____

_____

_____

_____

_____

_____

_____

_____

SPECIAL TIPS

Mid-South

LATE CAMELLIA SASAN-QUAS, MID-SEASON CAMELLIA JAPONICAS, WINTERSWEET (CHIMONANTHUS PRAECOX), JANUARY JASMINE, AND WINTER HONEYSUCKLE HAVE THE POTENTIAL TO BE IN BLOSSOM DURING THE MILD DAYS OF JANUARY.

Texas and the Gulf South

LOOK FOR PLANTS THAT ARE OUTSTANDING AT THIS TIME OF THE YEAR. AMONG THE BEST IS WINTER HONEYSUCKLE (LONICERA FRAGRANTISSIMA). THEIR CREAM-COLORED BLOOMS ARE UNBELIEVABLY FRAGRANT AND APPEAR ALL WINTER. WINTER HONEYSUCKLE IS A SHRUB THAT IS WELL ADAPTED TO ALL ZONES IN THE SOUTH AND HAS BEEN A FAVORITE FOR GENERATIONS.

Florida

THIS IS NORMALLY A DRY MONTH, WITH AN AVERAGE RAINFALL OF 2.2 INCHES FOR THE STATE. IN GENERAL, YOUR LAWN NEEDS ABOUT ³⁄₄ INCH TO 1 INCH OF WATER DURING THE SEASON. YOU MAY FIND A RAIN GAUGE HELPFUL IN MEASURING THE AMOUNT OF WATER THAT NATURE IS SUPPLYING.

_____

_____

_____

_____

_____

_____

_____

_____

_____

_____

_____

_____

_____

_____

_____

_____

_____

_____

_____

_____

_____

_____

_____

FOURTH PART OF THE MONTH

SPECIAL TIPS

Mid-South

DON'T BE CONCERNED ABOUT SPRING-FLOWERING BULBS COMING UP WHILE THE POSSIBILITY OF SEVERE COLD STILL EXISTS. THEY ARE HARDY AND WILL WITHSTAND SEVERE FREEZES. DO NOT MULCH OR COVER THEM. THIS ALLOWS THE BLOOM BUD TO COME UPWARD INTO THE FREEZE ZONE OF THE SOIL, WHERE FLOWER BUDS MIGHT BE DAMAGED.

DO NOT COVER PLANTS WITH PLASTIC DURING PERIODS OF SEVERE COLD. THEY WILL HEAT UP DURING SUNNY DAYS AND MAY DRY OUT AND BURN.

Texas and the Gulf South

CONTACT YOUR COUNTY EXTENSION AGENT FOR RECOMMENDATIONS ON SPECIFIC VARIETIES FOR YOUR AREA BEFORE SELECTING FRUIT TREES.

MANY PEOPLE FORGET ABOUT PLANT CARE IN JANUARY, BUT THIS IS A GOOD TIME TO PLAN THE COMING YEAR'S LAND-SCAPE OR EVEN THAT NEW DECK OR GARDEN POND YOU'VE HAD IN MIND. IF YOU HAVE BEEN THINKING ABOUT PUTTING IN VEGETABLES, THIS IS THE TIME TO CHECK OUT THE NEW CATALOGS. CHECK YOUR GARDEN SOIL'S PH AND GET IT PREPARED FOR NEW GROWTH. MOST VEGETABLES LIKE A PH BETWEEN 5.5 AND 6.9. IF YOUR SOIL'S PH (THE TERM FOR THE SOIL'S ACIDITY OR AKALINITY) IS TOO ACIDIC, ADD DOLOMITE AND IF IT'S TOO ALKALINE, ADD SULPHUR. HAVING THE CORRECT PH IS AN IMPORTANT FACTOR IN THE PRODUCTION OF QUALITY VEGETABLES.

Flowering quince is one of the showiest ornamentals of late winter and early spring. This native of Eastern Asia is well adapted to all but the southernmost parts of the South, where the lack of sufficient chilling can inhibit flowering. In addition to being exceptionally cold hardy, quince can tolerate our long, hot summers and periods of drought.

Many hybrids and forms of *Chaenomeles* exist, from dense, low-spreading bushes to large, lax shrubs. The most common form is a coral red color and ranges from 3 to 6 feet tall when mature.

Other colors include pink, white, and red. Bloom season usually begins with the first warm days of midwinter and can last for 4 to 6 weeks.

As early as mid-January, stems with buds can be taken indoors and placed in water in a warm window. Usually the buds will open and are attractive additions to the home at an otherwise bleak time. Since winter and spring are good times to shape and prune quince, don't feel guilty about cutting some to display indoors.

PLANT OF THE MONTH

JANUARY

FLOWERING OR JAPANESE QUINCE

(Chaenomeles speciosa)

William D. Adams

FEBRUARY

WHAT TO PLANT

Mid-South

February is really two gardening months; the first part is often the coldest part of the year and the second part brings the first hints of spring. Outside plantings for this month include: asparagus roots, horseradish roots, rhubarb roots, Jerusalem artichoke roots, Irish potatoes, Black-seeded Simpson lettuce seed, wrinkled English pea seed (including sugar snap types), garlic cloves, onion plants and sets, hardy annuals (pots or roots), hardy biennials (pots or roots), hardy perennials (pots or roots), sweet pea seed, bearded iris roots, peony roots, dormant fruit and nut trees (potted, balled, or bare-root), dormant fruiting vines (potted or bare-root), dormant bush fruits (potted, balled, or bare-root), evergreen shrubs (balled or potted), flowering shrubs (bare-root, balled, or potted), flowering trees (bare-root, balled or potted), shade trees (bare-root, balled, or potted), and vines (bare-root and potted).

For this month's inside planting, refer to January's list of hardy vegetables, flowers, and herbs. Also start seed for Bibb lettuce, leaf lettuces, and half-hardy annuals.

Texas and the Gulf South

February is an excellent time to plant bare-root and container-grown roses.

Plant dahlia tubers now (or in March) and sow seeds for nasturtiums, annual phlox, California poppies, coneflowers, and larkspur. Continue planting and transplanting shrubs and trees. Winter and early spring planting allows time for plants to become well established before hot weather arrives. Dig, divide, and plant summer- and fall-flowering perennials just before they initiate spring growth. Chrysanthemums, physostegia, Mexican marigold-mint, liatris, and fall-blooming salvias all respond to dividing and planting now. Mid-February to mid-March is potato planting time in the South. Cut up seed potatoes and allow them to dry for a day, or no less than a few hours, before planting.

Florida

Many northern bulbs do not grow well in Florida, but the amaryllis is one of the best flowering bulbs for our area. It is best when planted from October through this month. If you stagger the planting times, amaryllis will produce flowers from as early as March through May. Remember that amaryllis should be planted with one-third to one-half of the bulb above ground.

February usually stirs thoughts of Valentine's Day, but that's not all you should be thinking of this month. It's time to plant flowering annuals like petunias, pansies, marigolds, zinnias, nasturtiums,

geraniums, impatiens, begonias, nico-
tianas, pinks, phlox, and sweet alyssum
from seed. Many people like to plant roses
in February. Although bare-root roses
may seem like a bargain, you are better
off buying container-grown roses from
your local nursery. Roses that are container grown and grafted onto fortuniana
rootstock are better because their longevi-
ty is significantly increased. Bare-root
roses often die in a year or two; container-grown roses can last up to 50 years.
Pick a bright sunny location, amend the
soil, and plant them at the same depth
they were set at in the container.

FEEDING

Mid-South

The first part of the month, finish fertilizing all trees (including fruit trees). Fertilize pecans with a fertilizer containing
zinc. Fertilize summer-flowering shrubs
and trees.

The last part of the month, fertilize
and lime figs, fertilize evergreen lawns
and roses when they are pruned.

Texas and the Gulf South

Fertilize pansies, stock, poppies, larkspur,
and other cool-season annuals again with
about $1/2$ pound of ammonium sulfate per
100 square feet of bed area. Apply dried
blood meal to flowering plants.

Florida

Fertilize your lawns, fruit trees, shade
trees, and woody ornamentals—this is the
most important fertilization of the year
because the main growing cycle is just
about to begin. For your lawn, apply
16-4-8. The first number in the mixture
stands for nitrogen, which should notice-
ably augment your lawn's color and
growth. Phosphorus, the second number,
promotes good root formation and flowering, and potassium, the third number,
adds to the plant's over-all strength.
Fertilize citrus trees with a citrus special.
Often this number will be 4-6-8. Make
sure it contains minor elements and if it
doesn't, spray your trees with Minor-El
too. Even if the citrus special does include
minor elements, applying the nutritional
spray will not hurt your trees. For trees
and shrubs, apply a 6-6-6 or an 8-8-8
fertilizer. Normally apply $1/3$ cup per 2
to 3 feet of spread for shrubs. For trees
apply about 1 pound per inch of the
trunk's diameter.

About this time, most palms are hungry and will grow and look much better if
they are fed palm food. Extra manganese
and magnesium will also be helpful. One
common problem is frizzle top, which is
identified by twisted new growth. Manganese will control this problem.

GARDEN TASKS

Mid-South

Prune fruit trees, grapes, muscadines, and
scuppernongs. Prune summer-flowering
shrubs and trees. Prune roses at the end
of the month. Prune clematis back to the
main stems. Prune back liriope before the
new growth buds can be seen.

Finish dormant spraying in early
February. Remove all dead plant material
from beds, borders, vegetable gardens,
and shrub plantings. Remove old mulch
and replace with fresh new material.

Texas and the Gulf South

Prune everblooming roses during
February with good shears that make
clean cuts. Climbing and once-blooming
roses should be pruned after they bloom
in spring. Remove dead, dying, and
weak canes, but leave 4 to 8 healthy
ones. Remove approximately half of the
top growth and height of the plant. Wait

until they have finished flowering before pruning spring-flowering shrubs such as flowering quince, azaleas, and forsythia. When pruning shrubs, follow these steps: (1) prune out any dead or damaged branches first; (2) thin out by removing about one-third of the canes or stems at ground level, cutting out only the oldest canes; (3) and shape the rest of the plant but do not cut everything back to the same height. Pruning of evergreens and summer-flowering trees and shrubs should be completed in late February. Prune spring-flowering trees and shrubs as soon as they finish blooming. The ideal time to spray dormant fruit trees, pecans, and many ornamentals with dormant oil spray is just before budbreak.

Florida

Start preparations for your vegetable garden. First, pick an area that will get at least 6 hours of sun every day. Clear any rocks, stones, twigs, or debris from the area and have a pH test run on the soil. You may want to then sterilize the soil with Vapam. If you do this, stay at least 3 feet away from existing trees and shrubs and wait at least three weeks before planting. Many vegetables grow quickly, so you might want to plant some of your seeds each week in order to have a continuous supply of lettuces, radishes, and carrots.

Remove dead wood from your landscape, citrus, and other fruit trees. When trimming, make sure that the wounds are clean and that you leave a slight stub or shoulder when trimming. The cut should be fairly flush with the main trunk or branch. Seal the wound with pruning paint.

This is one of the best months to put out new plantings. But remember that our soil is so poor that in most cases the addition of extra organic matter, such as peat and cow manure, will create a better foundation for new plantings.

TROUBLESHOOTING

Texas and the Gulf South

Watch for pill bugs, snails, and slugs. They can damage tender cool-season annuals such as pansies. Apply chemical bug baits or lure them to their demise with small saucers of beer.

Florida

You may have noticed some brown spots on your lawn that start off small and then grow together, affecting large areas. This could be the beginning of brown patch fungus. To stop this problem, apply Dithane M-45, or any other good fungicide, following the directions on the label.

FIRST PART OF THE MONTH

SPECIAL TIPS

This is a good time to make cuttings of begonias, coleus, geraniums, and impatiens that are over-wintering in pots. Root the cuttings in perlite.

Don't fertilize newly planted trees or shrubs until they have started to grow, and then only very lightly for the first year. Fertilizer can burn the trees' and shrubs' vulnerable roots, causing them to die.

Florida

Frost may occur in northern Florida throughout most of this month. February 15 is normally the last killing frost in central Florida, but southern Florida may not have frost until after the first part of the month. Tender plants may still need to be protected with a light covering until the end of the month if a light frost is expected.

SECOND PART OF THE MONTH

_____

_____

_____

_____

_____

_____

SPECIAL TIPS

To give your carried-over plants a boost, fertilize them with a growing strength solution.

_____

_____

_____

_____

Remember that potted plants, trees, and shrubs make excellent Valentine's Day gifts.

_____

_____

_____

_____

Florida

Poinsettias will look a bit raggedy by now and will benefit from being trimmed back. These cuttings can be used to start new plants. About now your plant may be showing signs of scab—a wartlike cankerous growth that affects the stem and, sometimes, the foliage—and you may find that an application of Dithane M-45 will help it.

_____

_____

_____

_____

_____

_____

_____

_____

_____

_____

_____

_____

THIRD
PART
OF THE
MONTH

SPECIAL TIPS

Mid-South

APPLY PRE-EMERGENCE
WEED AND CRABGRASS
CONTROLS WHEN THE
FIRST FORSYTHIA BLOS-
SOMS ARE SEEN.

WHEN BUYING PLANTS,
BIGGEST IS NOT ALWAYS
THE BEST—ESPECIALLY
WITH BARE-ROOT
PLANTS. SMALL- TO
MEDIUM-SIZED PLANTS
(4 TO 6 INCHES HIGH)
ARE EASIER TO ESTAB-
LISH AND OFTEN QUICK-
LY OUTGROW LARGE-
SIZED ONES.

Florida

LAWNS CAN BENEFIT FROM POWER RAKING OR VERTI-CUTTING. THATCH IS CAUSED WHEN THE GRASS STARTS TO GROW OVER ITSELF. THE VERTICAL BLADES OF A VERTI-CUTTER REMOVE ABOUT ONE-THIRD TO ONE-HALF OF THE EXISTING GRASS. YOU MAY WISH TO HIRE A PROFESSIONAL TO DO THE WORK FOR YOU.

FOURTH PART OF THE MONTH

SPECIAL TIPS

Mid-South

PLANTS THAT ARE POTENTIAL FEBRUARY BLOOMERS ARE: MID-SEASON CAMELLIA JAPONICAS, FORSYTHIA, JANUARY JASMINE, FLOWERING QUINCE, WINTER HONEYSUCKLE (BUSH TYPE), EARLY SPRING-FLOWERING BULBS, AND ORIENTAL MAGNOLIA (IF THE WINTER IS MILD).

Texas and the Gulf South

TAKE TIME TO SMELL AND ENJOY THE OLD-FASHIONED VIOLETS (VIOLA ODORATA). THEY BLOOM WHEN LITTLE ELSE IS FLOWERING AND THEIR FOLIAGE MAKES THEM USEFUL AS BORDERS OR GROUND COVERS IN SHADED AREAS.

_____

_____

_____

_____

_____

_____

_____

_____

_____

_____

_____

_____

_____

_____

_____

_____

_____

_____

_____

_____

_____

_____

_____

_____

SINCE YOU HAVEN'T USED THAT OLD LAWN MOWER FOR THE LAST FEW MONTHS, YOU MAY WANT TO HAVE THE BLADE SHARPENED, CHANGE THE OIL, AND GIVE IT A TUNE-UP FOR SPRING.

PLANT OF THE MONTH

FEBRUARY

WINTER HONEY-SUCKLE

(Lonicera fragrantissima)

William C. Welch

Lonicera fragrantissima is no newcomer to southern gardens. It can be found growing unattended in old cemeteries and homesites where few other ornamental plants survive. The two most often used common names are winter honeysuckle and standing honeysuckle, both of which provide useful insight into the plant's landscape character. Robert Fortune, the great plant explorer from Scotland, found *L. fragrantissima* in China and introduced it into Europe in 1845. Soon thereafter, it appeared in American gardens.

The flowers are small and creamy white. They appear during midwinter and, although not outstanding in appearance, are highly fragrant.

Foliage is rounded and bluish green in color. In all but far South Texas and southern Florida, *L. fragrantissima* is deciduous and the flowers occur on bare branches. It is unusually well adapted and can be found throughout the South. Any good garden soil is sufficient; quality specimens have been found growing in either moderately alkaline or acidic soils.

Maximum height is about 8 feet with an arching form to the branches. Red fruit in spring will often follow the winter flowers. Landscape uses include specimens, background plantings, or hedges. Winter honeysuckle is very cold- and drought-tolerant. Propagation is from seed, cutting, or division of older clumps. *L. fragrantissima* is generally available nationwide and is often sold as a packaged deciduous shrub during winter.

Early southerners often placed a specimen of winter honeysuckle near a frequently used gate to the garden so that its fragrance and flowers could be easily enjoyed. Stems are also nice to cut and bring into the home where partially open buds continue to open.

Few plants will thrive in southern gardens with less attention.

WHAT TO PLANT

Mid-South

March brings the first signs of spring to the mid-South. The soft warm air moves from the lower part of the region northward as the month wears on. Bulbs come into bloom and the South's spring-flowering trees begin the annual show for which this part of the country is famous.

There is, however, one caveat. Frost is still a danger throughout most of the mid-South until April. Foolish is the gardener who plants tomatoes, zinnias, and other tender annual flowers and vegetables until all danger of frost has passed.

Plant asparagus roots, horseradish roots, rhubarb roots, Jerusalem artichoke roots, Irish potatoes, hardy vegetable plants (purchased from a nursery or raised indoors), hardy annuals (potted or roots), hardy biennials (potted or roots), hardy perennials (potted or roots), sweet pea seed, bearded iris roots, half-hardy annuals, dormant fruit and nut trees (potted, balled, or bare-root), dormant fruiting vines (potted or bare-root), dormant bush fruits (potted, balled, or bare-root), evergreen shrubs (balled or potted), flowering shrubs (balled or potted), roses (bare-root and potted), flowering trees (balled or potted), shade trees (balled or potted), and vines. Plant seeds of hardy vegetables like beets, carrots, collards, kale, lettuces (Bibb and loose-leaf types), mustard greens, sugar peas, radishes, rapegreens, spinach, and turnips. All evergreen lawn grasses, such as Kentucky bluegrass, Kentucky 31 fescue, turf-type fescue, creeping red fescue, chewing fescue, and *Poa trivialis* should also be planted now. March is the best month to plant *Magnolia grandiflora*.

It's a good idea to plant tender vegetables and annuals in indoor seed trays so they will be ready to plant in April when the danger of frost has passed. Good candidates for seed trays are eggplant, peppers, tomatoes, ageratum, sweet alyssum, amaranthus, aster, begonia, calendula, celosia, cleome (may also be seeded in beds in late April), coleus, cornflower, cosmos, dwarf dahlia, dianthus, dusty miller *(Cineraria)*, four o'clocks, gaillardia, gazania, gerbera (may also be planted from roots in April), geranium, gomphrena, heliotrope, annual hollyhock, impatiens, larkspur, lobelia, marigold, moonflower, morning glory, nasturtium, nicotiana, nierembergia, California poppy, Shirley poppy, petunias, portulaca, salvia, snapdragon, statice, sunflower, thunbergia, tithonia, torenia, verbena, vinca, and zinnia.

Texas and the Gulf South

Check with your county extension agent or local weather service to determine

the average frost date in your area. Be prepared to provide temporary protection for frost-sensitive transplants such as tomatoes, corn, peppers, geraniums, begonias, and coleus. Plant dahlia tubers in well-prepared beds and divide fall-blooming perennials such as chrysanthemums, physostegia, and *Salvia leucantha*. Petunias, zinnias, marigolds, celosia, and portulaca are good warm-season annuals for sunny locations. Choose from caladiums, coleus, impatiens, pentas, and fibrous-rooted begonias for partially shaded areas.

Florida

Begin thinking about planting flowers. Azaleas will be the queen of the landscape, but remember that they require a slightly acid soil. First-time azalea growers or those who may have had trouble growing them, should have a pH test run to determine their soil's acidity. If the acid is too high, use sulphur or a soil acidifier to lower the pH. Annuals you may consider planting include: floss flower (or ageratum), begonias, celosias, dahlias, Dahlburg daisies, marigolds, periwinkles, portulacas, wishbone flowers, verbenas, and zinnias. Caladiums, cannas, dahlias, day lilies, gloriosa lilies, and gladiola bulbs can also be planted now.

Everyone enjoys the natural beauty of roses and spring is a great time to plant them. Many good varieties will be available at your local nursery. Be sure to get varieties grafted onto the best rootstocks for Florida—'Dr. Huey' and 'Fortuniana.' Roses grow best where they get full sun for at least 6 hours a day. Add 25 pounds of peat, 25 pounds of dehydrated cow manure, and 2 to 3 pounds of a good quality fertilizer for every 100 square feet to the rose bed.

FEEDING

Mid-South

Finish fertilizing evergreen lawns. Fertilize all evergreen shrubs, roses (when you prune them), spring-flowering shrubs (as they finish blooming), and peonies (when their flower buds can be seen).

Texas and the Gulf South

Continue fertilizing pansies, larkspur, and other cool-season annuals with about 1.2 pounds of ammonium sulfate per 100 square feet of bed area. Fertilize trees and shrubs as they begin to grow. As azaleas and camellias finish blooming, fertilize them with azalea-camellia fertilizer, following the instructions on the label. Divide the recommended amount into three applications, to be done 3 to 4 weeks apart.

Florida

If you have not fertilized your lawn for the spring, this is a great time to get the job done. I usually use a 16-4-8 plant food. If your lawn needs thatching and you didn't do it last month, do it now.

All trees will benefit from being fertilized now. For a large tree, you might wish to use 1 pound of dry fertilizer, such as 6-6-6, per foot of tree spread, starting about 1 foot from the trunk and working out to the dripline (the perimeter of the tree's overhang).

GARDEN TASKS

Mid-South

Apply pre-emergence weed and crabgrass controls to your lawn and spray for weeds. Prune roses by early March. Prune evergreen shrubs—heavy pruning is alright—and spring-flowering shrubs when they finish blooming.

William D. Adams

Texas and the Gulf South

Finish pruning evergreens and summer-flowering trees and shrubs in early March. Spring-flowering trees and shrubs should be pruned as soon as they finish blooming. Select and order caladium tubers for April or May planting. Do not plant them until soil temperatures are about 70°F.

Florida

Cut back your grape plants if you have not already done so. They should be cut back to about 4 or 5 buds.

TROUBLESHOOTING

Mid-South

Watch for insects as the weather warms. Control them quickly to prevent a massive population increase. Work flower beds and vegetable areas whenever the soil is not too wet so they will be ready for planting at the right time.

Texas and the Gulf South

Scale, aphids, whiteflies, and spider mites become apparent as new foliage emerges. Dormant or summer oil sprays may be used until temperatures reach 85°F. or more. Insecticidal soaps are also effective. Watch for black spot and powdery mildew on roses and apply controls such as Funginex on a regular basis.

Florida

Many trees and shrubs may have been injured by the winter temperatures and may need to be cut back. Some people cut back too early, but by mid-March, you can usually start this operation. If you are not sure how far to cut back, take a pocket knife and start scraping along the outer wood near the tip of the branch, working your way back slowly until you see green wood in the cambium layer. This indicates good healthy wood; make your cut 4 inches beyond the point that the green wood starts.

FIRST
PART
OF THE
MONTH

_____
_____
_____
_____
_____

SPECIAL TIPS

_____

Mid-South

START TENDER BULBS
IN POTS INSIDE SO
THEY WILL BLOOM MORE
QUICKLY WHEN PLANTED
OUTSIDE ONCE THE
GROUND WARMS UP.

_____

TAKE TIME TO PARTICI-
PATE IN LOCAL GARDEN
TOURS AND TRAILS. IT
IS AN EXCELLENT WAY
TO GATHER USEFUL
IDEAS FOR YOUR OWN
GARDEN.

_____
_____
_____
_____
_____
_____
_____
_____

Florida

FOR EVERY DOLLAR INVESTED IN YOUR GARDEN, YOU SHOULD RECEIVE ABOUT 7 TO 10 DOLLARS IN FRESH VEGETABLES. BUT EVEN IF YOU ONLY BREAK EVEN, THE TASTE OF FRESH VEGETABLES GROWN IN YOUR GARDEN CERTAINLY MAKES THE EFFORT WORTHWHILE. MR. GREEN THUMB'S FAVORITE VEGETABLE GARDEN CHOICES INCLUDE: LIMA BEANS, POLE BEANS, CABBAGE, CUCUMBERS, EGGPLANT, MUSTARD, OKRA, PEAS, PEPPERS, RADISHES, AND TOMATOES.

SECOND PART OF THE MONTH

_____

_____

_____

_____

_____

_____

_____

_____

_____

_____

_____

_____

_____

_____

_____

_____

_____

_____

_____

_____

_____

_____

_____

_____

SPECIAL TIPS

Mid-South

THE FOLLOWING BULBS RESPOND WELL TO BEING STARTED INSIDE: ALOCASIA, TUBEROUS BEGONIA, CALADIUM, AND COLOCASIA (ELEPHANT'S EAR).

Texas and the Gulf South

START HANGING BASKETS OF PETUNIAS, FERNS, AND OTHER PLANTS TO GIVE YOUR GARDEN A DIFFERENT DIMENSION.

SEEDLINGS AND YOUNG PLANTS REQUIRE MORE CARE AND WATER WHEN FIRST GROWING. WITH SEEDS, THIS MEANS WATERING AT LEAST ONCE A DAY, AND MAYBE TWICE A DAY WHEN IT'S DRY AND WINDY OUTSIDE. AS THEY GROW OLDER, YOU MAY BE ABLE TO CUT BACK WATERINGS TO EVERY OTHER DAY.

THIRD PART OF THE MONTH

_____

_____

_____

_____

_____

_____

_____

_____

_____

_____

_____

_____

_____

_____

_____

_____

_____

_____

_____

_____

_____

_____

_____

_____

SPECIAL TIPS

Mid-South

PLANTS THAT CAN BE EXPECTED TO BLOOM IN MARCH INCLUDE: MID- TO LATE-SEASON CAMELLIA JAPONICAS, FORSYTHIA, SPRING-FLOWERING BULBS, ORIENTAL MAGNOLIA, STAR MAGNOLIA, YOSHINO CHERRY, FLOWERING PEACH, FLOWERING PEAR, FLOWERING PLUM, REDBUD, AND SPIREA (EARLY FLOWERING TYPES).

BEWARE OF CLOSE-OUT SALES ON BARE-ROOT TREES AND SHRUBS. THEIR CHANCES FOR SURVIVAL THIS LATE IN THE SEASON ARE VERY SLIM. INSTEAD, SELECT CONTAINER-GROWN AND BALLED-AND-BURLAPPED PLANTS.

Florida

VEGETABLES GROW BEST WHERE THEY GET A GOOD DEAL OF FLORIDA SUNSHINE. GENERALLY, THEY REQUIRE 5 OR 6 HOURS OF SUN A DAY. THIS IS ESPECIALLY TRUE OF SUN-LOVERS LIKE TOMATOES, PEPPERS, EGGPLANTS, AND POTATOES. PLANT LEAFY VEGETABLES SUCH AS CABBAGES, BRUSSEL SPROUTS, LETTUCES, AND GREENS IN THE SEMISHADY AREAS OF YOUR GARDEN. VEGETABLES PREFER A PH OF 5.5 TO 6.5, SO A SOIL TEST SHOULD BE YOUR FIRST STEP. BECAUSE OUR FLORIDA SAND HAS ABOUT 1 PERCENT ORGANIC MATTER, YOU CAN SEE THAT LARGE AMOUNTS OF COMPOST, PEAT, AND OTHER ORGANIC MATTER ARE NEEDED.

FOURTH PART OF THE MONTH

SPECIAL TIPS

COVER YOUNG SEEDLINGS WITH SHEETS OF NEWSPAPER IF THE TEMPERATURE SHOULD DROP BELOW 32°F.

WHEN FERTILIZING, IT IS NOT NECESSARY TO PUNCH HOLES IN THE GROUND TO FERTILIZE TREES AND SHRUBS. SURFACE APPLICATION HAS BEEN SHOWN TO BE MORE EFFECTIVE AND MUCH EASIER. BE SURE TO WATER WELL AFTER APPLYING.

Florida

MANY OF YOUR SHRUBS WILL BENEFIT FROM REMULCHING NOW. PLANTS SUCH AS PODOCARPUS, PITTOSPORUM, AND LIGUSTRUM MAKE EXCELLENT HEDGE PLANTS—THIS IS A GOOD TIME TO SET THEM OUT.

Louisiana irises are native to the Gulf Coast, where the soil is rich and there is plenty of humidity and moisture. Unlike most other iris family members, Louisianas actually thrive in boggy conditions, even when partially inundated for long periods. They do not, however, require these conditions and grow well in most any good garden soil. Moist conditions during winter and early spring are usually sufficient.

Louisiana irises like rich, highly organic soils. A winter application of composted manures or balanced fertilizer increases its spring flowering. The Louisianas are native to the deep South; the garden varieties are derived from *Iris brevicaulis*, *I. fulva*, and *I. giganticaerulea*. The Abbeville irises, native to a small area near that Louisiana city, are classified as unique, and giant *I. fulvas* are probably the most important of the collected species. They have huge flattened flowers in many shades of red and yellow. The broad range of colors available in the Louisiana irises even exceeds those of the tall bearded iris.

Fall, winter, and spring are their primary growing seasons. Hot, dry conditions in summer will induce a dormancy that seems to cause little, if any, harm to the plants.

Louisiana irises are among the more useful perennials as landscape plants. Their foliage is tall, up to 4 feet high, and handsome. Flowers occur in spring and work well at the rear of a perennial border or at the edge of a garden pond or lake. Dividing the plants in the fall every 3 or 4 years is a helpful, but not essential, cultivation practice and is also the major means of propagating the plants.

PLANT OF THE MONTH

MARCH

LOUISIANA IRIS

William C. Welch

GROWING YOUR
OWN GROCERIES

The home vegetable garden has always been an integral part of southern gardening. It was born out of necessity during hard times and has continued as vegetable production areas become more and more remote. The song "Home Grown Tomatoes" illustrates one of the best reasons why vegetable gardening has remained so popular over the years. There is nothing better than a home grown tomato! Freshness, high quality, and vine-ripe flavor are but a few of the reasons for having a vegetable garden— but they are also the most important ones.

What is a vegetable garden supposed to be? Actually, it can be anything the gardener wants. A hanging basket with a Tiny Tim tomato, a Celebrity tomato in a tub on the patio, sweet or hot peppers in a flower border, eggplant in the flower garden, bush beans as a border, a 10' by 10' plot of intensely planted vegetables, or a half-acre of carefully planned vegetable plantings all qualify as vegetable gardens. You really only need a sunny, well-drained garden spot and some planning.

Vegetables demand little to produce well. A sunny location is required with at least six hours of full sun per day. Good drainage is extremely important. Vegetables, with very few exceptions, do poorly when their roots are in wet, sticky soil. Obviously vegetables, like most garden plants, need well-prepared, friable soil that has the basic nutrients for the plants to grow and develop. Finally, vegetable plants need care. Insects and diseases must be controlled, weeds have to be prevented from competing for water and nutrients, and vegetables need proper moisture.

Take out the word "vegetables" and substitute "flowers" and the rules are almost exactly the same except for the absolute necessity of full sun. Many flowering and foliage plants do quite well in shade but not vegetables. Otherwise, good gardening practices make good vegetable gardens just like they make good flower gardens.

PLANNING THE VEGETABLE GARDEN

1. Choose a sunny, well-drained part of your yard.
2. Decide what vegetables to grow and whether to start with plants. Then choose whether or not to grow these plants from seed at home ahead of time or to purchase them at a nursery at planting time.
3. Find out whether they are cool-season or summer vegetables to determine when to plant each one.
4. Determine the length of harvest. Some vegetables, like sweet corn and

melons, mature at once and must be harvested in one or two weeks. Others like tomatoes, peppers, and eggplants may be harvested for many months. In between, there are those like squash, okra, and pole beans that produce for many weeks but not all season.

5. Decide how many plants or rows will provide the amount of any one vegetable needed. There is nothing more discouraging than to have zucchini by the bushels or enough okra to supply all of New Orleans' gumbo.

6. Make a garden plan. Lay out one area for cool-season vegetables, another for summer crops. The summer area should be subdivided into an area for full-season crops, another for crops that are harvested for many weeks, and then an area for crops that are harvested all at once.

PREPARING THE SOIL

Good soil preparation is essential to success with vegetables. Work the soil deeply and pulverize it thoroughly. Tilling is the easiest way, but you can use a spading fork to repeatedly turn the soil in small areas. Work dolomitic limestone and compost or another source of humus into the soil. Prepare soil ahead of planting time when it is dry. Working wet soil may be harmful to its structure.

PLANTING

Most vegetables are best planted on raised beds. This is essential for root crops such as beets, carrots, and potatoes and is also advisable for general crops. These beds prevent roots from being in soil that is too damp and developing poorly. Beds should be about two feet across for general crops and three feet for potatoes.

The distance between rows varies with the type of vegetable and method of cultivating. Mechanical cultivation with a tiller is easy but requires row spacing wide enough for the tiller to work without damaging the beds.

Your seed packets suggest the spacing between plants in the row, but don't try to sow seed to this spacing. It is better to sow more thickly and thin out young plants than it is to have skips in the row when some seeds don't germinate.

Before seeding, open a 3- to 4-inch-deep furrow down the center of the bed. Place a 5-10-15 fertilizer in this small furrow and work it in with a pointed hoe. Then place the seed in the furrow and cover to the depth indicated on the packet.

GROWING THE CROP

It takes fertilizer, water, insect and disease control, and control of weeds to produce good vegetables. Sidedress with 5-10-15 fertilizer every four to six weeks during the growing and harvesting time. Place the fertilizer in a band on each side of the row of plants on the bed and lightly work it in with a three-prong cultivator.

Water thoroughly when there is no rain for one week. Use a sprinkler and apply an inch of water at a time. Place a pound coffee can halfway between the sprinkler and the end of the fall of water. Run the sprinkler until there is an inch of water in the can.

Gardens can be kept free of weeds either by cultivation or mulching. It is easy to hoe out weeds in small gardens but difficult in larger ones. Tillers are excellent cultivators and are easy to use. Mulching plants is also an excellent way to control weeds, especially on long-standing crops. Dry grass clippings from the lawn are good and make excellent humus when turned under after the crop.

Insects and diseases often damage vegetables. Keep a watchful eye and dust or spray as soon as the first ones are seen. **Be sure and read the label on pesticides.** They will always tell the time between the last application and safe harvesting.

HARVESTING

Vegetables are better out of the garden because they can be harvested at their prime and eaten immediately. However, sometimes it is hard to know when they reach their most flavorful condition. Here are some general rules:

Asparagus:	when smaller than the little finger
Beans:	before the bean seed bulges in the pod
Beet:	when 1½ inches across
Broccoli:	when the head is tight and bright green
Cabbage:	when the head is tight
Cantaloupe:	when the stem pulls evenly off the melon
Carrots:	when the top of the root is less than 1 inch
Cauliflower:	while the head is still bright white
Collards:	while the leaves are young and soft
Sweet corn:	when the silks are brown
Cucumber:	while still deep green
Eggplant:	when fruit is large and dark purple

Lettuce, leaf or butterhead:	as soon as large enough to eat
Lettuce, head:	when the heads are firm
Mustard greens:	while young and tender
Okra:	under 5 inches long
Onion, bulbs:	when tops break over
Onion, green:	anytime when large enough
English peas:	when peas are young
Pepper, sweet:	when pods are large but still green
Pepper, hot:	when bright red and still shiny
Squash, yellow:	while small and slick-skinned
Tomato:	when fully red
Watermelon:	when the tendril by the stem is dead and it thumps deeply
Zucchini:	while still slick green and under 7 inches

VEGETABLE GARDENING TIPS

- Use an 8-inch single-drain-hole flower pot to distribute fertilizer down the row or when sidedressing: Fill the pot with fertilizer, keeping a finger under the drain hole. Release the finger at the beginning of the row and walk rapidly down the row allowing fertilizer to flow from the drain hole.

- Stake tomatoes when they are planted. Staking them later may damage their roots.

- Keep rabbits from eating young vegetable leaves by hanging small mesh bags filled with human hair every 4 feet round tender young plants, especially sprouting beans.

- Bright yellow strips of plastic covered with a tacky material will attract and kill whiteflies.

- Bury large plastic buckets—like those that spackling compound comes in—between tomato plants. Drill a series of holes in the base of the bucket. Keep filled with a fertilizer solution. Tomatoes will flourish and produce enormous crops.

- Don't worry if the first flowers of cucumber, zucchini, and squash fall off without setting fruit. These are male flowers. The female or fruiting flowers will come later and produce good fruit.

- Plant pepper and eggplant after the weather warms. Plantings in cool weather are attacked by flea beetles.

- Do not plant sweet corn too early. Wait until the ground warms. Sweet corn seed will rot in cold damp ground.

- Southern cowpeas make an excellent summer green manure/cover crop in bare areas after harvest of early vegetables. Till under before the stems become woody.

WHAT TO PLANT

Mid-South

April is the height of spring in most of the mid-South. Three great groups of plants—dogwood, azalea, and camellia—combine to bring as much beauty to the garden as you'll find anywhere. They provide inspiration to be out in the garden working—even those who never do more than cut the lawn will become avid gardeners this month.

The month is divided into three parts: when frost danger still exists, when the danger of a freeze has passed but the ground is still cool, and when frost season is over and the ground has warmed. Plant beets, carrots, lettuces (set plants for Bibb and loose-leaf types), mustard greens, radishes, rapegreens, spinach, turnips, half-hardy annuals, fruit and nut trees (potted or balled), fruiting vines (potted), dormant bush fruits (potted or balled), evergreen shrubs (balled or potted), flowering shrubs (balled or potted), roses (potted), flowering trees (balled or potted), shade trees (balled or potted), and vines (potted) during the first part of April.

Once the chance of a freeze is over, but while the ground is still cool, plant bush snap beans, pole beans, canteloupes, cucumbers, summer squash, tomato plants, zucchini, Kentucky bluegrass,

Kentucky 31 fescue, turf-type fescue, creeping red fescue, chewing fescue, *Poa trivialis.* Plant bush lima beans, pole lima beans, Swiss chard, sweet corn, eggplant, okra, peppers, sweet potatoes, pumpkins, New Zealand spinach, baking squash, watermelons, tender annuals (potted or roots, except zinnias), tender perennials (potted or roots), common Bermuda grass (seed or sod), hybrid Bermuda grass (sod), carpet grass (seed), centipede (seed or sod), St. Augustine (sod), and zoysia (sod).

Texas and the Gulf South

Container-grown and balled-and-burlapped trees and shrubs are at their peak of availability now. Annuals and perennials are also in strong supply and respond well to transplanting this month. April is an ideal time to seed Bermuda grass lawn areas as well as to plant St. Augustine, zoysia, and centipede grass sod. Amaranthus, cosmos, portulaca, and zinnia seeds can still be planted this month, but you must keep seeded areas moist until the seeds germinate. Thin out the plants as soon as they are large enough to transplant and share the surplus with friends and neighbors. For instant color, purchase started plants in 4- or 6-inch containers. Plant caladiums as soon as ground temperatures reach approximately 70°F. Southern peas, okra, corn, cucumbers, and squash may now be direct seeded in the garden. Continue planting tomato, eggplant, and pepper plants.

Florida

Many of the spring flowers can be planted now, but remember that most flowers need 6 hours of sun every day. Sweet potatoes are delicious and make an attractive ground cover too. They need a long growing period, so now is the time to plant them. Planting is as easy as buying a sweet potato at the supermarket, placing toothpicks in it, and resting it in a cup of water to root. Once rooted, you can either cut up the potato or cut up some of the green sprouts and plant them in your garden.

FEEDING

Mid-South

Fertilize summer grass lawns. Finish fertilizing evergreen shrubs. Feed roses every 6 to 8 weeks and fertilize spring-flowering shrubs, azaleas, and camellias as they finish blooming.

Texas and the Gulf South

Roses have a high fertilizer requirement. Use a complete fertilizer for the first application just as new growth starts, then use ammonium sulfate every 4 to 6 weeks, usually just as the next growth cycle starts following flowering. Apply water-soluble fertilizer to hanging baskets and other container plants every 2 to 3 weeks.

Florida

Annuals are heavy feeders. After planting, fertilize lightly with a good water-soluble plant food every 3 to 4 weeks.

GARDEN TASKS

Mid-South

Prune spring-flowering shrubs, azaleas, and camellias when they finish blooming. Spray fruits until they are ripe. Follow the schedule recommended on the product's label.

Texas and the Gulf South

Thinning peaches increases fruit size, improves fruit color and reduces limb breakage. The earlier they are thinned the better.

Start weeding early. Competition from weeds can delay desirable plants' flowering and fruiting. A 2- or 3-inch layer of mulch will discourage weeds amd make those that do come through easier to pull.

Florida

Now is the time to resod some of those barren spots in your lawn. Another less expensive option is to plug bad areas. The most common plugs are made from St. Augustine varieties. If you have a bahia lawn, you can over-seed with bahia grass seed and it should germinate now that the temperatures are warmer. When seeding, remember to keep the soil moist or you risk losing the seed. Apply 1 inch of water each week when rainfall is infrequent. Verti-cutting can still be done this month if you have not yet fertilized.

TROUBLESHOOTING

Mid-South

Watch for insects this month. You must act quickly to control them or infestation will radically increase. To keep the weeds in your lawn from becomimg uncontrollable, apply a dry or liquid weed killer.

Texas and the Gulf South

Watch for the first signs of powdery mildew on crape myrtles and roses and apply Funginex or other controls if any appears. Sooty mold on gardenias is an indication that whiteflies are present. Orthene or insecticidal soap works well to eliminate them. Thrips are tiny insects that damage or destroy flower buds of roses, irises, and many other plants. They particularly like light-colored flowers. If you find aborted or damaged blossoms, tear apart a bloom and look closely for these tiny pests' movement. Apply Orthene, Diazinon, or other materials labeled to control them.

Florida

You may notice your gardenias are looking yellow or that the Ixora has green veins or a yellowish cast. This is a sign of a deficiency. Many of the minor elements, such as iron, copper, zinc, and manganese are just not present in Florida's soil. If they are present, the pH may prevent them from being absorbed. If in doubt, apply a nutritional spray such as Minor-El.

Figs are grown throughout the state and in many northern states as well. In general, they are shrublike, but can become tree-sized. Two varieties recommended for Florida are Celeste and Brown Turkey. Figs, like many of our Florida plants, respond well to a good layer of mulch. On occasion, they have problems with rust, which is a fungal disease. To treat this problem, apply a neutral copper with each flush of new growth.

MOST SUMMER BULBS MAY BE PLANTED THIS MONTH AFTER THE GROUND WARMS AND WHEN THERE IS NO DANGER OF FROST. HERE ARE SOME OF THE FAVORITES:

NAME	ALSO CALLED	LOCATION
AGAPANTHUS	LILY OF THE NILE	FULL SUN
ALOCASIA	FANCY ELEPHANT'S EAR	PART SHADE
BEGONIA (TUBEROUS)		LIGHT SHADE
CALADIUM		PART SHADE
CALLA LILY		LIGHT SHADE
CANNA		FULL SUN
COLOCASIA	ELEPHANT'S EAR	LIGHT SUN
CRINUM	MILK AND WINE LILY	FULL SUN
DAHLIA		FULL SUN
GLADIOLUS		FULL SUN
GLOXINA		LIGHT SHADE
HEDYCHIUM	GINGER LILY	LIGHT SHADE
HYMENOCALLIS	SPIDER LILY	LIGHT SHADE
IRIS, BEARDED	FLAG OR GARDEN IRIS	FULL SUN
TUBEROSE		FULL SUN
WATSONIA		FULL SUN

FIRST PART OF THE MONTH

SPECIAL TIPS

PLANT VEGETABLES ON BEDS (RIDGES) FOR GOOD DRAINAGE.

TO FULLY UTILIZE FLOWER OR VEGETABLE SEEDS LEFT OVER FROM PLANTING, CLOSE THE PACKETS WITH TAPE OR A PAPER CLIP AND STORE THEM IN A SEALED GLASS JAR OR AIRTIGHT PLASTIC BAG IN YOUR REFRIGERATOR. MANY SPECIES CAN BE SAVED FOR A YEAR OR MORE IN THIS MANNER.

SECOND PART OF THE MONTH

SPECIAL TIPS

Mid-South

WATCH FOR AZALEAS, LATE SEASON CAMELLIA JAPONICAS, SPRING-FLOWERING BULBS, KWANZAN CHERRIES, DOGWOODS, SPIREA (LATE BLOOMING TYPES), AND VIBURNUM TO BLOOM THIS MONTH.

REMOVING SPENT FLOWERS, TRIMMING BACK EXCESSIVE GROWTH, AND APPLYING FERTILIZER TO ESTABLISHED ANNUALS CAN DO WONDERS TO REJUVENATE A PLANTING.

Florida

GERANIUMS ARE ONE OF THE BRIGHTEST SPRING BLOOMERS WE HAVE. TO KEEP THEM FLOWERING AT THEIR BEST, PINCH OR CUT OFF THE OLD FLOWER HEADS AS THEY BEGIN TO FADE. THIS WILL HELP THE PLANTS TO CONTINUE PRODUCING FLOWERS AND LOOKING ATTRACTIVE.

THIRD PART OF THE MONTH

SPECIAL TIPS

Mid-South

APRIL IS A GOOD MONTH TO START A REGULAR SPRAY SCHEDULE FOR ROSES.

Texas and the Gulf South

PRUNE BACK CLIMBING ROSES AS SOON AS THEY COMPLETE THEIR FLOWERING. BEGIN BY REMOVING DEAD OR WEAK CANES, THEN SHORTEN OTHERS AND THIN VIGOROUS TYPES ABOUT ONE-THIRD.

Florida

ALTHOUGH NORTHERN
PEACH VARIETIES DO
NOT DO WELL IN FLORI-
DA, THE FLORIDA BELLE
PRODUCES PEACHES
THE SIZE OF BASEBALLS
THAT TASTE LIKE ANY
NORTHERN PEACH.
OTHER VARIETIES FOR
FLORIDA ARE FLORIDA
ONE, FLORIDA BEAUTY,
AND FLORIDA GOLD.
ANOTHER VARIETY THAT
HAS BEEN AROUND FOR
A LONG TIME IS THE RED
CEYLON. PEACHES MAY
NOT LIVE AS LONG AS
SOME FRUIT TREES, BUT
YOU SHOULD STILL
ENJOY MANY, MANY
YEARS OF GOOD PRO-
DUCTION FROM THEM.

FOURTH PART OF THE MONTH

SPECIAL TIPS

Texas and the Gulf South
REMOVE FADED BLOOMS FROM PANSIES AND FERTILIZE LIGHTLY TO EXTEND FLOWERING INTO MAY.

Florida

Although most people do not think of growing apples in Florida, there are several varieties that do quite well here. Anna and Ein Shemer, developed by the Israelis, and Golden Dorset, introduced from Nassau, Bahamas, require very few chilling hours and can be grown successfully in our state.

PLANT OF THE MONTH

APRIL

NASTURTIUM

(Tropaelum majus)

Distinctive appearance, rapid growth, and easy culture characterize this once-popular annual. Nasturtiums contain mustard oil, which is why their flower buds and young fruits are used for seasonings and are sometimes pickled. Unripe seedpods have a peppery flavor, somewhat like watercress, and may also be used in salads.

Nasturtiums are grown as cool-season, temperate plants. In the South the seed is usually planted about the time of the last frost. They should be planted where they can be allowed to mature because young seedlings can be difficult to transplant. Seedlings started in small individual pots indoors or in the greenhouse can, however, be set out earlier and, therefore, provide a longer bloom season.

Nasturtiums are native to the cool highlands from Mexico to central Argentina and Chile. There are both climbing and dwarf bush types.

The dwarf types are much more commonly available and are useful as 10- to 12-inch tall borders or mass plantings in sun or partial shade. Their flowers range in color from creamy white to orange, mahogany, red, and yellow. Double-flowered forms are also available.

Nasturtiums do better in well-drained soil with moderate to low fertility. The seeds are large and sprout quickly. In most of the South, they bloom until really hot weather begins, which is usually in June.

The climbing or trailing kinds can quickly cover fences, banks, or stumps, and are excellent in the winter greenhouse as a source of cut flowers or ornamentals. The flowers have an unusual and refreshing fragrance.

Nasturtiums are susceptible to few insects or diseases and add a touch of old-fashioned charm as potted specimens, mass plantings, or borders in vegetable gardens. They are also a good choice to mix with spring-flowering bulbs because they effectively hide the unattractive bulb foliage that must be allowed to mature. Nasturtiums are at their peak of flowering during May and June. If you have not grown them before, look for places now where they can be planted early next spring.

William C. Welch

WHAT TO PLANT

Mid-South

With May comes the end of cold weather throughout the mid-South; frost danger passes in the higher elevations and summer gardening is in full swing. Many gardeners plant their flower beds, borders, and planters now. Hanging baskets are abundant in nurseries this time of year. These old-fashioned additions to porches and outdoor living areas lend unique beauty to their settings throughout the season.

Watch the weather this month because May starts out like a continuation of April, but by mid-month it may be very dry. This is our second driest month of the year, so be prepared to irrigate lawns and gardens.

All vegetables that were planted in April may still be planted this month. Plant vegetables that require warm soil to perform, including: bush lima beans, pole lima beans, Swiss chard, sweet corn, eggplant, okra, peppers, sweet potatoes, pumpkins, New Zealand spinach, baking squash, and watermelons. Also plant all tender summer and fall bulbs and tender flowering plants, including those like zinnias that require warm soil to grow well.

May is the ideal time to plant summer grasses like Bermuda grass, centipede, St. Augustine, and zoysia. It is too late to plant fescue and other cool-season grass-es. From May until November, container-grown trees, shrubs, and fruits may be planted even though it is not generally recommended. If you do plant them, you must be extra diligent about watering during dry periods.

Texas and the Gulf South

Early May is the ideal time to plant caladiums. Plant them in partially shaded areas in well-prepared soil that is high in organic content. Consider planting fast-growing vines on a trellis, fence or an overhead structure. Select from hyacinth bean, jack beans, morning glories, moon vine, black-eyed susan, or gourds. They all like sunny locations and a structure for support. Perennial vines can also be spectacular. Consider coral vine, Dutchman's pipe, and sweet autumn clematis. Continue planting zinnias, portuluca, marigolds, and cosmos. It is finally hot enough to plant two favorite hot-weather annuals: globe amaranth and periwinkle. Perennials that should be planted now include cannas, achimenes, lantana, purple coneflowers, salvias, and lythrum. Herbs are also available and are interesting when interspersed with annual and perennial borders. Rosemary, Mexican marigold-mint, and society garlic (Ulbaghia) are as handsome as any other hot-weather plant and have culinary value too. Continue planting container-grown trees and shrubs. Okra, sweet

potatoes, and southern peas may also be planted now.

Florida

Cherry tomatoes can still be planted and will produce fruit throughout the warmest months. Okra, southern peas (such as black-eyed peas), sweet potatoes, collard greens, and quick-maturing vegetables (like radishes and leafy lettuces) can all still be planted.

FEEDING

Mid-South

Fertilize summer grass lawns and finish fertilizing evergreen shrubs. Feed roses every 6 to 8 weeks. Fertilize spring-flowering shrubs, azaleas, and camellias once they have finished blooming.

Texas and the Gulf South

Continue adding small amounts of nitrogen fertilizer to annuals, perennials, and roses.

Florida

May ushers in our warmer months. Roses will be in full bloom, and camellias will be blooming as well. Geraniums will have red flowers, marigolds will be awash in yellow, and gerberas will have beautiful bright red and yellow flowers. This is an important time to fertilize them—as summer approaches, your shrubs, vines, and trees become hungry.

If your St. Augustine or bahia lawn is starting to look yellow, it may simply need fertilizing. Folks tend to forget to fertilize their lawns in early spring—you need to remember that lawns are growing plants. Apply a balanced plant food and continue to watch for chinch bugs. In your St. Augustine, their presence may first appear as a yellow or brown spot near the street or driveway and in your bahia as a soft, spongy area. Treating with Diazinon, Dursban, or Oftanol should minimize damage.

GARDEN TASKS

Mid-South

Prune spring-flowering shrubs, azaleas, and camellias when they finish blooming. Spray fruits until they are ripe, following the schedule on the product's label. Continue a spray schedule for roses—this will control black spot, which is the worst disease to strike during May, and thrips, which can be especially serious when the weather is dry. Keep the weeds in your lawn controlled and irrigate lawns and gardens whenever necessary as the weather becomes dry and hot.

Texas and the Gulf South

Prolong the flowering season and tidy the garden by removing old blossoms on spring-flowering annuals and perennials. Be sure that newly planted trees are staked to prevent wind damage. Now that freeze damage from the past winter can be assessed, crape myrtles and other ornamentals can be cut back to live wood. Make cuttings of your favorite chrysanthemums and root them in a mixture of sand and peat moss. Cover the cutting box with plastic and place it in a shaded area for 5 or 6 days to prevent wilting. Cuttings should be adequately rooted in 3 to 4 weeks and ready to set in the garden.

Florida

Eventually all trees must be trimmed, but this does not mean they should be butchered or topped. It is usually best to hire a professional to handle a large trimming job, not only so it is done properly but also to avoid the dangers of falling branches. During the hurricane season, it is advisable to check trees for diseased

William D. Adams

areas that denote weakened limbs. It is well worth a horticulturist's fee to have your trees examined periodically so you can keep them in top condition.

TROUBLESHOOTING

Mid-South

Keep a vigilant watch for insects and diseases and start control measures immediately to prevent extensive damage. Watch for lacebugs on azaleas. They are found on the underside of the leaves, which look mottled. Brown residue on a leaf's underside is a sure sign of their presence. Other insects that attack ornamentals are spidermites, spittlebugs, leafhoppers, scale, and Japanese beetles (near the end of the month).

As for your lawn, keep an eye out for chinch bugs. Brownpatch may also be a problem on thick-turf lawns; it can be controlled with a lawngrass fungicide. Watch for the following insects in the vegetable garden:

- aphids—on all vegetables, especially greens

- corn earworm—on the ears, inside the silk and husk

- cabbage green worm (looper)—on cabbage, cauliflower, and broccoli

- striped cucumber beetle—on cucumber, squash, and zucchini

- fleabeetle—on peppers, eggplant, and, occasionally, on tomatoes

- squash vine borer—on squash, zucchini, and cantaloupes

- Mexican bean beetle—on all types of snap and lima beans

- thrips—on beans and squash

Texas and the Gulf South

Watch for wilting with new trees and shrubs. Water every 3 or 4 days and mulch to reduce soil temperature and water evaporation. Watch for spider mites and aphids.

Florida

As the heat increases, so do the outdoor and indoor pests. Carefully check the underside of your indoor plants' leaves for pests. Mites are often a problem. You may want to use a hand lens to check for them. They are tiny—only about $1/50$ of an inch in size—and are closely related to true spiders. You may first notice a stippled appearance on the leaf or you may find a small bit of webbing. To treat mites, spray the plant with Malathion, Cygon, or Orthene, following the directions on the label. Respray in 5 days to catch the second generation. Other creatures that attack our indoor plants are aphids, mealy bugs, and scales. These can be controlled with the same sprays used to control mites.

FIRST PART OF THE MONTH

_____
_____
_____
_____
_____
_____
_____
_____
_____
_____
_____
_____
_____
_____
_____
_____
_____
_____
_____
_____
_____
_____

SPECIAL TIPS

COOL-SEASON VEGETA-
BLES ARE READY TO
HARVEST: BROCCOLI,
CABBAGE, CAULIFLOWER,
ROOT CROPS, LETTUCE,
PEAS, AND SPINACH.

ALLOW FOLIAGE OF
SPRING-FLOWERING
BULBS TO MATURE
AND YELLOW BEFORE
REMOVING BECAUSE IT
ENABLES THEM TO
STORE UP ENOUGH
ENERGY TO BLOOM
NEXT YEAR.

Florida

ONE OF THE BIGGEST
DIFFERENCES BETWEEN
GARDENING IN THE
NORTHERN STATES AND
GARDENING IN FLORIDA
IS THE NUMBER OF
TROPICALS THAT CAN
BE USED IN OUR LAND-
SCAPES. IN FACT, MANY
NORTHERNERS COUNT
THE DAYS UNTIL THEY
CAN RETIRE IN FLORIDA
AND PLANT THAT FIRST
HIBISCUS, BIRD-OF-PAR-
ADISE, CROTON, COPPER
PLANT, OR TROPICAL
PALM. WHEN PLANTING
TROPICALS, KEEP IN
MIND THAT PLANTS
PLACED NEAR A WALL
OR CLOSE TO YOUR
HOME WILL HAVE MORE
PROTECTION FROM THE
COLD THAN THOSE
PLANTED IN THE MIDDLE
OF YOUR YARD OR ON
THE NORTH SIDE OF
YOUR HOUSE.

SECOND PART OF THE MONTH

_____
_____
_____
_____
_____
_____
_____
_____
_____
_____
_____
_____
_____
_____
_____
_____
_____
_____
_____
_____
_____
_____
_____

SPECIAL TIPS

HYDROCOOLING ALL COOL-SEASON VEGETABLES INCREASES THEIR KEEPING QUALITY. TO DO THIS, FILL YOUR SINK WITH WATER THAT HAS BEEN CHILLED WITH MANY ICE CUBES. PLUNGE THE VEGETABLES IN THE COLD WATER AND LEAVE THEM THERE FOR AT LEAST 10 MINUTES BEFORE DRYING AND REFRIGERATING THEM.

Texas and the Gulf South

REPLACE OR REPLENISH MULCH MATERIALS IN FLOWER BEDS AND SHRUB BORDERS TO CONSERVE MOISTURE AND REDUCE WEED GROWTH.

THIRD PART OF THE MONTH

_____

_____

_____

_____

_____

_____

_____

_____

_____

_____

_____

_____

_____

_____

_____

_____

_____

_____

_____

_____

_____

SPECIAL TIPS

Mid-South

WATCH FOR LATE (SAT-SUKI) AZALEAS, EARLY RHODODENDRON, AND ROSES TO BLOOM THIS MONTH.

Texas and the Gulf South

PINCH BACK TERMINAL GROWTH ON NEWLY PLANTED ANNUALS AND PERENNIAL PLANTS TO ENCOURAGE MORE COMPACT, BETTER BRANCHED PLANTS AND MORE FLOWERS.

Florida

AZALEAS AND GAR-
DENIAS SHOULD BE
TRIMMED OR PRUNED TO
BRING THE PLANTS BACK
INTO SHAPE. BY TRIM-
MING THE DOMINANT
BUD YOU WILL GET
MORE LATERAL BUDS TO
SPROUT. THIS WILL GIVE
YOU A BUSHIER PLANT
AND MORE POTENTIAL
BLOOMS. IF YOU HAVE
NOT ALREADY DONE SO,
TRIM BACK YOUR POIN-
SETTIAS. NEW SHOOTS
THAT DEVELOP SHOULD
BE TRIMMED AGAIN
WHEN THE POINSETTIAS
ACHIEVE 1 FOOT OF NEW
GROWTH.

FOURTH PART OF THE MONTH

_____

_____

_____

_____

_____

_____

_____

_____

_____

_____

_____

_____

_____

_____

_____

_____

_____

_____

_____

_____

_____

_____

SPECIAL TIPS

RABBIT DAMAGE MAY BE A SERIOUS PROBLEM ON EMERGING BEANS AND YOUNG LETTUCE. A GOOD WAY TO DIVERT THEM IS TO PLACE SMALL MESH BAGS FILLED WITH HUMAN HAIR AROUND THE GARDEN.

Texas and the Gulf South

BRIGHTEN A SHADED AREA OF THE GARDEN WITH PENTAS, BEGONIAS, CALADIUMS, AND IMPATIENS.

CRAPE MYRTLES ARE
ONE OF THE PRETTIEST
PLANTS, AND ARE
OFTEN SHOWCASED IN
LANDSCAPES. THEY ARE
A GOOD SUBSTITUTE
FOR THE NORTHERN
LILAC. ONE OF THE
MAJOR PROBLEMS THEY
HAVE DURING THE
SUMMER MONTHS IS
POWDERY MILDEW. TO
COMBAT THIS PROBLEM,
SPRAY THE PLANTS WITH
A FUNGICIDE (READ THE
LABELS TO FIND ONE
USED FOR THIS PROB-
LEM).

Yarrows are aromatic perennials useful in borders and rock gardens. Another common name for them is sun fern, which describes both their appearance and their preference for high light intensity.

Yarrows are native to northern temperate areas and have naturalized in many parts of the United States, including the South. Dried flowers and leaves have been used medicinally, primarily to treat wounds. The flattish flower heads are popular for use in dried floral arrangements.

The white-flowering yarrow is most common, although dark pink, lavender, and yellow cultivars are available. Culture is easy and requires only routine care—water moderately, cut back bloom stems after flowering, and divide when clumps get crowded. Few insects or diseases attack yarrow. They respond to good soil and fertilizer, but will tolerate fairly stressful conditions.

Propagation is usually by division, although seed can produce flowering-size plants the second year. Availability is good; most seed catalogs and perennial growers offer some cultivars.

The long bloom season, which may last from spring through fall, and the fernlike foliage make yarrows useful and interesting plants. Their fine texture, ease of culture, long bloom season, and usefulness as dried material have made yarrows a staple item with knowledgeable gardeners.

PLANT OF THE MONTH
MAY

YARROW
(Achillea millifolium)

William C. Welch

WHAT TO PLANT

Mid-South

June brings the mid-South's first real summer weather. It is generally hot with afternoon thundershowers. This month's high humidity creates ideal conditions for insects and diseases, which must be controlled as soon as they are noticed because extensive plant damage occurs rapidly. Most cool-season vegetables have now been harvested, which leaves room in the garden for second plantings of sweet corn and beans.

Continue planting warm-season vegetables. Most warm-weather flowers may still be planted; plant chrysanthemums for fall bloom. Continue planting dahlias and gladiolus. Now is an excellent time to seed or sod summer grasses, such as Bermuda grass, centipede, St. Augustine, and zoysia.

Texas and the Gulf South

Hot-weather vegetables such as melons, southern peas, eggplant, and squash may still be planted in June. Colorful annuals like zinnias, cockscomb, periwinkle, salvia, and cosmos can be started from seeds or transplants. Copper plant and Joseph's coat *(Alternanthera)* are two outstanding fall foliage plants that are best planted now. Container-grown nursery trees, shrubs, vines, and ground covers may be planted all summer if they are properly watered when dry.

Florida

Plant crape myrtles while they're still in bloom and you can see each plant's flowers. Crape myrtles are the closest option to the northern lilac that Florida gardeners have.

FEEDING

Mid-South

Fertilize summer grass lawns. Feed roses every 6 weeks. This is the last call to fertilize azaleas, camellias, and dogwoods.

Texas and the Gulf South

June is a good time to run a soil test. Contact your county extension agent for further instructions. If it's not convenient to run a soil test, continue applying small amounts of nitrogen—about $1/2$ pound ammonium sulfate per 100 square feet—to planting areas every 4 to 6 weeks for the rest of the growing season. Water thoroughly after applying.

Florida

The general rule for feeding citrus is to fertilize in February, June, and October. Use a citrus special at the rate of 1 pound per foot of tree spread. Make sure to stay at least 1 foot from the trunk and apply the majority of the fertilizer under the dripline. As a supplement, apply a nutritional spray to the foliage a couple of times during the season.

Don't forget about feeding your other plants as well. Fertilize apple, avocado, mango, and fig trees and don't overlook oak trees.

GARDEN TASKS

Mid-South

Irish potatoes should be ready to harvest this month. Dig when the tops begin to die and the ground cracks around the stems. Onions are ready to dig when the tops break over and the ground has cracked around them.

Water lawns thoroughly during dry periods. Watch for chinch bugs and control them quickly. Cut Kentucky 31 fescue and the new turf-type fescues at least 3 inches high. Japanese beetles emerge in droves this month. Spray plants and treat lawn areas to control their grubs.

Shape and trim evergreens. Spray fruits until they are ripe, following the schedule recommended on the product label. Peaches and plums are particularly susceptible to brown rot disease.

Continue a regular spray schedule for roses. Black spot is the worst disease to plague them during June, and, again, thrips can be especially serious when the weather is dry.

Texas and the Gulf South

Pick cucumbers, squash, corn, beans, and other quickly ripening vegetables frequently to ensure their crispness and tenderness. Frequent picking will also prolong the harvest season.

Florida

Many of our most commonly used landscape plants, such as azaleas, camellias, and gardenias, prefer slightly acidic soil with a pH below 7.0. In fact, the average plant prefers a pH of 5.5 to 6.5. You should be checking your soil's pH at least every 6 months. If the pH level is not right, your plants may get chlorosis, which is characterized by a yellowing of the leaves. Many products are available to temporarily correct this problem. Iron sulphate can be applied at a rate of $1/4$ to $1/2$ pound per 10 square feet. Ordinary agricultural sulphur may also be used to correct chlorosis. However, the more finely ground dusting or wettable sulphurs

work better. Apply the sulphur at the rate of 1 pound per 100 square feet and do not use it more than 2 or 3 times per year. Wait at least 2 months between applications. Chelated iron compounds are also used to correct chlorosis. They can be applied to the foliage as well as the soil. Because the iron chelates are effective in relatively small amounts, an overdose may injure the plants. Be sure to follow label directions carefully.

TROUBLESHOOTING

Mid-South

Examine your ornamentals for these insects: lacebugs, leafhoppers, scale, spidermites, spittlebugs, and Japanese beetles.

Texas and the Gulf South

Bagworms can nearly strip junipers, arborvitae, and other evergreens. Use Diazinon, Orthene, Sevin, or Malathion after removing as many bags as possible. Webworms in pecans and many other trees are also troublesome at this time of the year and can be controlled with the same pesticides.

Florida

Many insects are active this month. It has been estimated that we get up to 1 million mole crickets per acre in badly infested areas. Many people use mole cricket bait to control the pests, and this is the best time to apply it. Set out the bait after a rain or when you have irrigated well, but never before a rainstorm because the rain will wash away the insecticide, leaving the bait and attracting more mole crickets. Bahia grass is the most likely to be attacked, although damage can occur to Bermuda grass and occasionally even to St. Augustine.

FIRST PART OF THE MONTH

_____

_____

_____

_____

_____

_____

_____

_____

_____

_____

_____

_____

_____

_____

_____

_____

_____

_____

_____

_____

_____

_____

SPECIAL TIPS

Mid-South

CRAPE MYRTLES, RHODODENDRONS, ROSES, AND CHASTE TREES (VITEX AGNUS-CASTUS) WILL ALL BE BLOOMING THIS MONTH.

ADDING 1 OR 2 TEA-SPOONS OF LIQUID DETERGENT TO SPRAY SOLUTIONS HELPS PESTICIDES STICK TO THE FOLIAGE AND PROVIDE BETTER COVERAGE.

TO KEEP YOUR VEGETABLES PRODUCING, PROMPTLY HARVEST RIPENED OR NEARLY RIPENED FRUIT BECAUSE YOUR PLANTS WILL CONTINUE TO PRODUCE AS LONG AS THE FRUIT ISN'T ALLOWED TO DEVELOP PAST MATURITY.

SECOND PART OF THE MONTH

_____

_____

_____

_____

_____

_____

_____

_____

_____

_____

_____

_____

_____

_____

_____

_____

_____

_____

_____

_____

_____

_____

_____

SPECIAL TIPS

Mid-South

LAWNS AND GARDEN AREAS MAY NEED WATERING IN JUNE. WATER THOROUGHLY; NEVER GIVE THEM JUST A SPRINKLE. TRY TO APPLY AT LEAST $1/2$ INCH OF WATER EACH TIME YOU IRRIGATE. TO MEASURE A SPRINKLER'S WATER OUTPUT, PLACE A 1-POUND COFFEE CAN HALFWAY BETWEEN THE SPRINKLER AND THE WATER'S FARTHEST-REACHING AREA. AFTER WATERING, MEASURE THE AMOUNT THAT HAS COLLECTED IN THE CAN TO DETERMINE HOW MUCH WATER HAS BEEN APPLIED. MOST PLANTS NEED AN INCH OF WATER PER WEEK.

Texas and the Gulf South

JUNE IS A GREAT TIME TO SELECT DAYLILY CULTIVARS BECAUSE MANY ARE AT THEIR FLOWERING PEAK.

Florida

GARDENERS OFTEN REPORT THAT THEIR VEGETABLES (ESPECIALLY TOMATOES, PEPPERS, AND SQUASH) LOOK GOOD ONE WEEK AND THEN TEND TO FADE. TYPICALLY, THE PLANTS' BOTTOM LEAVES TURN YELLOW AND BROWN AND THEN THE PLANT DIES. THIS IS CAUSED BY A FUNGAL DISEASE AND CAN BE TREATED BY SPRAYING WITH A FUNGICIDE. YOU MAY WANT TO CONSIDER SPRAYING PREVENTATIVELY BECAUSE THE HUMIDITY IN OUR STATE CAUSES CONSTANT FUNGAL PROBLEMS IN THE GARDEN.

THIRD PART OF THE MONTH

_____

_____

_____

_____

_____

_____

_____

_____

_____

_____

_____

_____

_____

_____

_____

_____

_____

_____

_____

_____

_____

SPECIAL TIPS

Mid-South

GARDEN AREAS THAT ARE BARE AFTER HARVESTING SHOULD BE PLANTED WITH COWPEAS AS A GREEN MANURE/COVER CROP. THESE SOIL-BUILDING LEGUMES GROW WELL IN HOT WEATHER AND WILL ADD NITROGEN AS WELL AS HUMUS TO THE SOIL. TURN THEM UNDER BEFORE THEY PRODUCE PEAS AND WHILE THE STEMS ARE STILL SUCCULENT.

Texas and the Gulf South

PINCH BACK ESTABLISHED CHRYSANTHEMUMS TO ENCOURAGE BRANCHING AND MOUNDING.

Florida

HANGING BASKETS PRO-
VIDE INTERESTING FOCAL
POINTS IN ANY ROOM
DECOR AND ARE IDEAL
FOR DISPLAYING
ASPARAGUS FERNS,
ENGLISH BABY TEARS,
IVIES, PATHOS, AIR-
PLANE PLANTS, AND
PIGGYBACK PLANTS.
FOR PLANTS WITH LONG
TRAILING VINES, A
HANGING BASKET IS THE
ONLY PRACTICAL WAY TO
PROVIDE IT WITH NEAR
NATURAL GROWTH CON-
DITIONS. MANY PEOPLE
PLACE HANGING BAS-
KETS IN STAIRWELLS,
BUT NO PLANT WILL SUR-
VIVE IN AN AREA WITH-
OUT WINDOWS, UNLESS
IT RECEIVES 14 TO 16
HOURS OF ARTIFICIAL
LIGHT DAILY.

FOURTH PART OF THE MONTH

_____
_____
_____
_____
_____
_____
_____
_____
_____
_____
_____
_____
_____
_____
_____
_____
_____
_____
_____
_____

SPECIAL TIPS

Mid-South

PINCH THE SHOOTS OF CHRYSANTHEMUM PLANTS WHEN EACH ONE IS 4 TO 6 INCHES LONG. THIS KEEPS PLANTS LOW AND BUSHY AND ENABLES THEM TO SET MORE BUDS.

Texas and the Gulf South

CRAPE MYRTLES RESPOND WELL TO A LIGHT APPLICATION OF COMPLETE FERTILIZER AS THEY BEGIN THEIR FLOWERING SEASON.

Florida

WATCH FOR BLACK SOOTY MOLD ON PLANTS. IT INDICATES A PEST PROBLEM—USUALLY APHIDS OR WHITE-FLIES—BECAUSE THEY EXCRETE A SUGARY WATER SOLUTION CALLED HONEYDEW THAT THE MOLD GROWS ON. YOU MAY SEE IT ON THE PLANT ITSELF, OR ON ITS FOLIAGE. TO TREAT, SPRAY WITH A GENERAL INSECTICIDE, SUCH AS DIAZINON, ORTHENE, OR MALATHION.

Larkspur have naturalized in some areas of the South and are known for their tall spikes of blue or purple flowers. Pink, white, and double forms are also available, but the seeds seem to revert to the dark blue, or purple, single form after a few years.

Spectacular and easily grown, larkspur is a fall-seeded annual that prefers to be left in place after germination. A sunny location and well-drained soil of moderate fertility are its major requirements. Thinning the seedlings in midwinter until they are 8 to 10 inches apart will usually yield a more impressive display of individual plants that reaches 3 to 5 feet tall. Like poppies and other annuals planted in the fall, larkspur usually need little supplemental irrigation because they complete their life cycle during our naturally cool, moist seasons.

Whether the seed is collected or allowed to fall and germinate naturally in the garden, it is important to remember that modern hybrid varieties often do not come true from open-pollinated seed. Seed saved from many of these modern types may have little resemblance to the original flower. Large and double flowers may return as small single ones and bright colors tend to become more muted.

Since larkspur respond well to cultivation and fertilization, it may be necessary to work the soil and add organic material and fertilizer after the seed has fallen.

PLANT OF THE MONTH

JUNE

LARKSPUR

(Delphinium grandiflora)

William C. Welch

This cultivation process may destroy some of the seed that has been planted too deeply, but a sufficient number usually remains to provide plenty of plants for the next season.

PLANTING FRUIT TREES

by Stan DeFreitas

Citrus can be very satisfying fruit trees to grow. Some citrus trees get quite large—grapefruit trees can grow to 40 feet. Orange trees, like the Navel, Hamlin, and Valencia, are more prone to grow 25 to 30 feet in height. Lemons and limes tend to be more bushlike, but can grow to be small-tree sized. The following list notes the most popular varieties and their harvesting times:

Oranges
Hamlin—October through January
Navel—October through January
Parson Brown—October through January
Pineapple—December through February
Valencia—March through June

Grapefruits
Duncan—November through May
Foster—November through March
Marsh—November through May
Ruby Red—November through May
Thompson Pink—December through May
Star Ruby—December through May

Limes
Key—October through December
Tahiti—February through November

Lemons
Ponderosa—December through March
Meyer—December through March

Following simple guidelines when planting citrus (or any other trees) will ensure that your new trees get the right start. First, choose a location where the soil has good drainage. (If you do not not have such a spot in your garden, plant the tree on a raised mound of soil that has been ammended with peat and dehydrated cow manure. For an adequate base, the mound should be 6 inches high and 8 feet across.) Begin by digging a hole that is two to three times as wide and twice as deep as the tree's rootball. The hole should be deep enough to handle even the longest root. If the tree appears to be root bound, gently pull the roots apart. This will allow the roots to extend out and down into the ground as the tree grows.

Before you refill the hole, mix the soil with peat or cow manure. Although there is some controversy about doing this, improving the quality of the soil can only have a positive effect on a tree's production and overall health.

Set the tree at the same depth in the hole as it was growing at in the container. This is very important because planting a tree too deep will often stunt its growth. If you are unsure, keep in mind that it is always better for a tree to be planted too shallow than too deep. Refill the hole with the amended soil mixture, adding water and making sure that there are no air pockets.

VERTICAL GARDENING

by Dr. William C. Welch

If your garden seems to have a terminal case of mediocrity, consider that you might need to add some vertical interest. Part of the excitement achieved by many of the world's greatest gardens is that the visitor cannot see the entire garden at once. There is a pleasant anticipation in moving from one room or area to another. You can use this concept in your own garden, no matter how small or large.

Forming these rooms can be done with walls of stone, brick, wood, or with living materials such as evergreen hedges. Another possibility is to use permanent structures designed to support roses or other vines. These can take the forms of walls, trellises, arches over entrances, pergolas, or garlands, which were popular during the heyday of Gertrude Jekyll, the famous English gardener of Victorian times.

Jekyll was a great believer in roses on structures and offered some very creative ideas on how they can be incorporated into the garden in her book, *Roses for English Gardens.* She further encouraged the use of species and old rambling roses, varieties known to be hardy and easily maintained. Broad walkways partially covered by wooden or metal structures were beautifully softened by roses selected for their graceful growth habits as well as the fragrance and beauty of their flowers. The vertical element, along with an inspiring awareness of texture and color,

was always strongly present in her planting designs.

Few modern roses are as graceful and as easy to cultivate as the old species and ramblers that inspired some of Jekyll's gardens. Fortunately, some of her favorites are once again available and well adapted to the South. Most grow quickly and can produce dramatic effects in as little as two years from time of planting.

Some of the best choices are once-bloomers. This means that the vine blooms only during the spring. The once-bloomers are some of the lovliest members of the genus. The fact that they bloom once, and then rest or grow, often mean that they are hardier, lower maintenence plants. Remember that climbing roses should usually be pruned *after* they bloom. Harsh pruning is not necessary for most plants; removing their weak canes and shaping them is all they need. My experience with own-root old roses verifies the tradition of their being planted with success by generations of southern gardeners. Most varieties seem to live longer and grow better when propagated from cuttings. The following are known to be successful in most areas of the South and are traditional favorites.

Species and Species Hybrids (all once-bloomers)
'Lady Banks Rose,' yellow and white
'Cherokee,' single white

Rosa Multiflora 'Carnea,' clusters of small, double pink flowers
Rosa × Fortuniana, double white
Rosa multiflora 'Platyphylla,' also known as 'Seven Sisters,' clusters of pink, purple, and white flowers

Repeat-flowering Climbing Roses
'Mermaid,' pale yellow single flowers
'Lamarque,' double white small flowers
'Jeanne d'Arc,' double white small flowers
'Zépherine Drouhin,' cerise flowers on thornless stems; mainly in spring
'Sombreuil,' formal creamy white double blossoms
'Cl. Cécile Brünner,' the "Sweetheart Rose," small double salmon pink

Roses are not the only vines that add vertical interest to southern gardens. Wisteria, Carolina jessamine, Dutchman's pipe *(Aristolochia elegans)*, coral *(Lonicera sempervirens)* and Heckrotti honeysuckles, coral vine *(Antigonon leptopus)*, and sweet autumn clematis are all famous for garden pictures they create. These vines are relatively permanent additions to the garden and require little more than periodic pruning and general garden care.

Another category of vines often overlooked in the garden are annuals. Our ancestors appreciated annual vines for their ability to provide quick shade and color. A traditional favorite is hyacinth

William C. Welch

bean *(Dolichos lablab)*, which Thomas Jefferson planted at the end of his vegetable garden each year. Vertical structures, which were made of locally gathered saplings, coupled with a fabulous display of hyacinthlike purple flower and seed pods in late summer and fall create a never-forgotten image.

Morning glories, moon vine, black-eyed susans, and various gourds can all create garden interest only a few months after they have been planted from seed. Seeds from these plants can be saved from year to year, making them economical as well as attractive additions.

Incorporating fruiting vines into your garden is still another way of combining plants and structures to create vertical interest. Blackberries, raspberries, and grapes can all be used for this purpose if you select adapted southern cultivars. 'Dormand Red' raspberries, 'Champanel' and 'Black Spanish' grapes, and various muscadines are well adapted. 'Brazos' and 'Rosborough' blackberries are dependable fruiting plants that can climb 5- to 6-foot structures in one season.

Increasing a garden's interest with vines and vertical structures is a technique that is part of a strong historical tradition and great aesthetic potential for today's southern gardens. Whether you choose roses or annual or perennial vines, the choices are many and the effects can be sensational.

WHAT TO PLANT

Mid-South

Hot weather in our part of the country is the norm this month. Temperatures soar and plant problems are compounded when there is rain in addition to the heat. However, it may also be dry and watering is absolutely necessary to keep flowers, lawns, and vegetables growing well. New plantings last winter and spring should be observed for signs of drought damage and soaked thoroughly if tip-wilting occurs.

July is not generally considered a good planting month. It is too hot for most shrubs, trees, fruits, flowers, and vegetables. The exception is summer grass planting, which may still be done with excellent results.

Texas and the Gulf South

Seeds for the following annuals may be planted now to bring color to your summer and fall gardens: marigold, zinnia, periwinkle, petunia, cosmos, portulaca, and ageratum. Late July is also a good time to start seeds for broccoli, cauliflower, cabbage, and other cole crops. Plant pumpkins now for Halloween. Tomato transplants should be set out as soon as possible for fall harvest. Shading the new plants will help them survive the first few weeks. In spite of the heat, it's not a bad time to move large live oaks and other trees and shrubs, but it is essential to keep transplants well watered until they become established. Many plants become semidormant with the summer heat, which makes them easier to move.

Florida

You can still plant some of those summer vegetables, such as cherry tomatoes, sweet potatoes, cowpeas, collard greens, leaf lettuce, and radishes. Oversummering of vegetables can be done by watering more and by planting leafy vegetables under partial shade.

Want some summer color in your garden? Plant marigolds, zinnias, portulaca, and many other summer flowers from seed. Be sure to water them every day. Sometimes sprinkling a bit of peat moss over the seeds will help keep them moist, which aids with germination. Remember that annuals live, flower, and die in one season and should be fertilized monthly with a water-soluble plant food. Other summer flowers you might want to try are cockscomb (Celosia), salvia, and vincas.

FEEDING

Mid-South

Continue feeding every six weeks. Summer grasses should be kept growing rapidly with high-nitrogen fertilizers every 6 weeks. Fruiting vegetables need a

1-2-2 ratio fertilizer during production peaks.

Texas and the Gulf South

Fertilizing is helpful for most plants at this time of the year, but it is important to water immediately after every application. Water-soluble fertilizers mixed according to label instructions are best for plants in containers and hanging baskets.
Florida

Don't forget to feed your annual flowers, bahia lawngrasses, bananas, blueberries, bromeliads, cacti, succulents, and heavy feeders such as papayas, figs, and St. Augustine lawngrasses.

GARDEN TASKS

Mid-South

Keep vegetables cleanly picked to encourage more production. Remove spent flowers and dead flower stalks to encourage more blossoms on your summer flowers. Harvest blueberries as they ripen. Keep lawns thoroughly soaked during the hot, dry weather.

It is too late to prune most spring-flowering trees and shrubs; they have already started setting bloom buds for next year's flowers. Evergreens can be trimmed, but don't do drastic pruning. Don't forget to control insects and diseases on all plants as soon as you see them.

Texas and the Gulf South

Pinch the tips out of copper plants, Joseph's coat, and chrysanthemums to encourage branching and, eventually, the development of more flowers. To keep plants in hanging containers looking attractive, soak the baskets in a tub of water every few days in addition to regular daily watering. This is also a good

time to fertilize baskets. Never apply fertilizer to dry plants.

Florida

This is the last month to prune back your azaleas, trimming them back at least one-third. It's also a good time to remulch azaleas with 2 to 3 inches of cypress mulch or wood chips. Remulching will help keep weeds to a minimum and will cause azaleas to use less water. Poinsettias often need to be trimmed back during July as well. Gardeners should trim off at least 1 foot of new growth. By doing this, you will end up with bushier plants that have more bracts (flowers) next season.

TROUBLESHOOTING

Mid-South

Worms are particularly bad this month. Watch for them on vegetables and flowers, especially on tomatoes, peppers, and geraniums. Bacillus thuringiensis (BT) is a very safe and effective control.

Cover bunch grape vines and blueberries with netting to prevent bird damage as the fruit ripens. Do not cut cool-season grasses too low. Low cutting will damage this type of grass plant. Recommended heights are:

Kentucky 31 fescue and turf-type fescues—3 to $3^1/_2$ inches high

Creeping red and chewing fescue—$1^1/_2$ to 2 inches high

Bluegrass—2 to $2^1/_2$ inches high

Texas and the Gulf South

Brown discolored foliage on junipers and marigolds may be caused by red spider mites. Hold a sheet of white paper below a branch and tap the branch sharply. If the dirt specks start to move, you can almost be certain you have spider mites.

Spray them with insecticidal soaps or a chemical labeled for control.

Florida

One common problem with figs is a fungus called rust. (The fungus gets its name from the rust color of the spores.) Fig rust can defoliate the fig. The infection begins as small yellowish spots that later enlarge and turn brown. It is best, as with most fungal diseases, to remove the infected leaves. This is especially true if you remove them before the spores are produced, preventing future disease outbreaks. Rake up the fallen leaves and spray each flush of new growth with neutral copper.

FOR THOSE WHO WOULD LIKE TO MAKE THEIR OWN SOIL MIX, COMBINE THE FOLLOWING MATERIALS IN EQUAL PORTIONS, USING PEAT MOSS, HUMUS, OR LEAF MOLD (THEY ARE INTERCHANGEABLE), AND YOU WILL HAVE A GOOD GARDEN AND POTTING SOIL:

VERMICULITE—A VERY LIGHT, MICA-LIKE MINERAL THAT HAS BEEN EXPANDED BY EXTREMELY HIGH HEAT. ITS POROSITY ALLOWS IT TO HOLD WATER LIKE A SPONGE, AND ALSO ENABLES IT TO IMPROVE A HEAVY SOIL'S DRAINAGE. A STERILE MEDIUM, IT CAN BE USED TO START SEEDS OR ROOT CUTTINGS.

PERLITE—A WHITE, STERILE MEDIUM THAT HAS BEEN PRODUCED FROM THE HEAT-INDUCED EXPLOSION OF VOLCANIC ROCK. ITS ROUGH EDGES WILL HOLD WATER, THOUGH NOT AS LONG AS VERMICULITE. PERLITE IS RECOMMENDED AS A GOOD ADDITION TO A SOIL MIX FOR PLANTS THAT PREFER TO BE KEPT ON THE DRY SIDE. PERLITE IS A GOOD ROOTING MEDIUM FOR SUCCULENT STEMS THAT TEND TO ROT IF GIVEN TOO MUCH MOISTURE.

SAND—FINELY GROUND PARTICLES OF STONE QUARTZ. COASTAL SAND WILL IMPROVE THE DRAINAGE OF ANY SOIL AND IS A NECESSARY COMPONENT IN A SOIL MIX FOR GROWING CACTI. SAND IS ALSO ONE OF THE BEST MEDIUMS FOR ROOT CLIPPINGS.

LEAF MOLD—PARTIALLY DECAYED LEAVES, USUALLY OAK LEAVES. LEAF MOLD IMPROVES THE QUALITY AND FERTILITY OF ANY SOIL AND IS ONE OF THE BEST SOURCES OF ORGANIC MATERIAL.

HUMUS—DECAYED VEGETATION THAT INCREASES THE SOIL'S WATER ABSORPTION. HUMUS ALSO IMPROVES THE QUALITY AND FERTILITY OF THE SOIL.

PEAT MOSS—THE DECOMPOSING REMAINS OF PLANTS. SPHAGNUM MOSS IS BY FAR THE BEST TYPE OF PEAT, SINCE IT RESISTS FURTHER DECOMPOSITION. PEAT HAS GOOD WATER-RETENTION PROPERTIES AND HELPS LIGHTEN THE SOIL'S TEXTURE.

FIRST
PART
OF THE
MONTH

SPECIAL TIPS

Mid-South

KEEP GARDEN AREAS
MULCHED WITH GRASS
CLIPPINGS OR PINE
STRAW TO CONSERVE
MOISTURE AND PREVENT
WEEDS.

Texas and the Gulf South

CHECK PLANTS FOR
MULCH AND REPLACE
OR ADD AS NEEDED.

_____
_____
_____
_____
_____
_____
_____
_____
_____
_____
_____
_____
_____
_____
_____
_____
_____
_____
_____
_____
_____
_____
_____
_____
_____

Florida

As summer approaches, Florida lawns will have more problems. Many people think that mowing their lawns very low to the ground allows them to mow less often and is good for the grass. This is not true; lawn grasses can be severly injured by hot, summer sun when mowed too short. Try to mow often enough so that you are only removing one-third of the leaf blades. Most St. Augustine grasses should be 2 to 3 inches long after mowing. Warmer weather also brings more insects and fungal diseases and makes nemotode damage more noticeable. Pesticides, such as Dursban and Diazinon, can be very effective treatment when used properly. When applied improperly, they can harm people, pets, and wildlife.

SECOND PART OF THE MONTH

SPECIAL TIPS

Mid-South

PINCH SPRING-PLANTED CHRYSANTHEMUMS UNTIL MID-MONTH, THEN ALLOW BUDS TO SET FOR FALL BLOOM.

Texas and the Gulf South

GLADIOLUS CORMS CAN BE DUG, CURED, AND STORED AS SOON AS THE FOLIAGE TURNS BROWN.

Florida

TREES ARE ONE OF THE FIRST ITEMS YOU SHOULD CONSIDER PUTTING IN YOUR LAND-SCAPE. ALTHOUGH THEY ARE SLOW TO DEVELOP, TREES GIVE LAND-SCAPES A FOCAL POINT AND PROVIDE SHADE FOR YOU AND YOUR SHADE-LOVING PLANTS.

THIRD PART OF THE MONTH

SPECIAL TIPS

Mid-South

PLACE A PIECE OF PLAS-
TIC UNDER EACH CAN-
TELOUPE TO PREVENT
THE PICKLE WORM FROM
ENTERING THROUGH THE
UNDERSIDE.

Texas and the Gulf South

DON'T FORGET TO WATER
LARGE-LEAFED PLANTS
LIKE HYDRANGEA,
COLEUS, CALADIUMS,
AND CHRYSANTHEMUMS.
EVEN IN THE SHADE,
HOT DRY WINDS CAN
QUICKLY DEPLETE THEIR
SOIL'S MOISTURE.

Florida

SHRUBS ARE A VERSA-
TILE, DECORATIVE LAND-
SCAPE CHOICE. THEY
SOFTEN THE LINES OF
WIDE AREAS, CREATING
A NATURAL BALANCE
BETWEEN FLOWER BEDS,
LAWNS, AND TREES.
LIGUSTRUM AND VIBUR-
NUM ARE GOOD FOR
THIS PURPOSE AND CAN
BE GROWN AS STAN-
DARD SHRUBS OR
TRIMMED AS TREES.
BOUGAINVILLEA AND
ALLAMANDA CAN BE
ALLOWED TO GROW
AS VINING PLANTS OR
TRIMMED INTO SHRUB-
LIKE SHAPES. WHILE
EVERYONE ENVISIONS A
LANDSCAPED YARD OR
GARDEN IN ITS FINAL
FORM, REMEMBER THAT
IT OFTEN TAKES SEVER-
AL YEARS FOR SUCH
DREAMS TO TAKE
SHAPE.

FOURTH PART OF THE MONTH

SPECIAL TIPS

Mid-South

SPRAYING FRUITING AND FLOWERING PLANTS WITH A SOLUBLE OR LIQUID FERTILIZER DURING HOT, DRY TIMES WILL HELP THEM CONTINUE TO SET FLOWERS AND FRUITS.

Texas and the Gulf South

THIS IS A GOOD TIME TO ORDER SPRING-BLOOM-ING WILDFLOWER SEEDS FOR PLANTING IN AUGUST OR SEPTEMBER.

Florida

People often talk of overwintering in the north. In the South we have to worry about oversummering. This means helping plants survive the intense summer heat. To oversummer your plants, use a sprinkler system and water in the early morning, which is also a good way to make the water last. Mulching the plants with at least 3 inches of mulch will help them live through the heat.

_____
_____
_____
_____
_____
_____
_____
_____
_____
_____
_____
_____
_____
_____
_____
_____
_____
_____
_____
_____
_____
_____
_____
_____
_____
_____
_____

PLANT OF THE MONTH

JULY

GIANT ROSE MALLOW

(Hibiscus moscheutos)

The giant rose mallow has the largest flowers of any hardy perennial—some measure a foot across. Giant rose mallows are relatives of the native hibiscus found growing in the ditches of Louisiana and other Gulf South states. They are among the most spectacular and easily grown plants for use in borders.

Rich, moist soil and full sun produce the most vigorous growth, but mallows will tolerate light shade as well as less desireable soils. Giant rose mallows will flower from seed the first year if started very early in the spring. Favorite cultivars may be rooted from cuttings during the growing season.

Following the spring and summer growing season, the plants freeze back to the ground each fall. Old stems should be cut back to a height of several inches above the ground. New shoots emerge by midspring and the plants quickly develop handsome mounds of foliage and flowers by early summer. Individual flowers last only a day, but each plant may flaunt several or more flowers at once.

Colors include crimson, white, pink, rose, and others in between. Numerous seedling selections such as 'Southern Belle' and 'Frisbee' are offered in good seed catalogs.

William C. Welch

A Southern Gardener's Notebook

AUGUST

WHAT TO PLANT

Mid-South

Mid-South gardens have great difficulties in August. Dog Days are here and the weather is often miserably hot and either too wet or too dry. Weeds grow profusely and insects and diseases attack in droves, making it tough to keep plants productive and gardens neat.

Plant bush beans, garlic, greens (kale, mustard, and rape), onions, shallots, and turnips in the vegetable garden. Seeds for broccoli, cabbage, cauliflower, collards, Bibb lettuce, onions, and parsley can be planted in beds or seed trays. Also plant seeds for English daisies, pansies, and hardy biennials and perennials in beds or seed trays. Full-grown chrysanthemum plants can be planted now as well.

Texas and the Gulf South

There is still time to start seeds for broccoli, cauliflower, cabbage, kale, and other cole crops for fall and winter production. Beans, melons, potatoes, sweet corn, peppers, southern peas, eggplant, and okra can also be planted now. Plant seeds for pansies, snapdragons, sweet alyssum, cornflowers, stock, and calendulas this month. Select a place in the garden where seedlings will be protected from afternoon sun and can be watered daily. August is an ideal time to divide and reset clumps of bearded, Louisiana, and *spuria* irises.

This time of the year, daylilies also respond well to dividing.

Florida

You can still plant some of the heartier vegetables this month. Despite the heat, okra, cherry tomatoes, field peas, and mustard and collard greens will do fine when planted this August. But you may have to spray them with Captan or Dithane M-45 to control mildew or with Thuricide to control chewing insects.

FEEDING

Mid-South

Fertilize all lawns this month. Continue a rose feeding schedule and fertilize all long-standing vegetables and flowers. *Do not* fertilize broadleaf evergreens this late in the year.

Texas and the Gulf South

Continue applying a water-soluble fertilizer solution to plants in containers and hanging baskets. Mid-August is the recommended time to give roses an application of fertilizer to boost their fall flower production.

Florida

Continue to feed annuals, houseplants, vegetables, and porch and patio plants with a water-soluble plant food.

GARDEN TASKS

Mid-South

Pick southern pears before they yellow and fall from the trees. Continue harvesting blueberries. Always remove spent flowers to encourage more blooms. Harvest vegetables regularly—keeping them picked clean will encourage more fruit.

Keep lawns watered during dry weather. Rake out dying crabgrass when it turns purple. Remove bush berries' canes after they have finished fruiting. Encourage new canes by fertilizing the plants. Resume a spray program on apples as the fruit increases in size.

Texas and the Gulf South

Mid-August is an important time in the rose garden. Begin by removing dead canes, then shorten long stems by about one-third. Early fall pruning and fertilizing is most important for everblooming shrub-type roses. Climbers and once-blooming types can be lightly shaped at this time. Dividing spring-flowering perennials such as Shasta daisies, ox-eye daisies, and phloxes should be done between now and early November.

Florida

This is a perfect month to make plans for your vegetable garden. Select a bright sunny location and sterilize the soil with Vapam. This should be done at least 3 weeks before planting and must never be applied closer than 3 feet to the existing roots of trees and shrubs. You can increase Vapam's effectiveness by covering the fumigated area with plastic.

Transplanting palm trees is another task done for this time of the year. About now, you are probably mowing your lawn at least once a week. With our tough St. Augustine or bahia grass, you are probably dulling the blade a lot quicker than you think. Be vigilant about keeping the blade sharpened; more people lose lawns to dull blades than to insects and diseases.

TROUBLESHOOTING

Mid-South

Be on the lookout for spider mites and thrips this month. They will attack many different plants during the hot weather.

Texas and the Gulf South

Watch for plants to make sure the heat is not drying them out. This is especially critical for plants that were set out this year. Look for wilted or dull-colored foliage and water deeply, but not every day, for most plants.

Florida

August, being one of the hottest months, is when insects are most prevalent. Reapply pesticides for mole crickets, chinch bugs, sod webworms, and oleander caterpillars. Mites, which are not true insects, will also be in full attack when the heat is at its worst. They can reproduce a second generation in as little as 5 days. For this reason, a second pesticide application will undoubtedly be necessary.

FIRST
PART
OF THE
MONTH

SPECIAL TIPS

Mid-South

THIS IS THE BEST TIME
TO LOOK FORWARD TO
FALL AND START SEEDS
FOR FALL VEGETABLES
AND FLOWERS WHILE
MAINTAINING THOSE
PLANTS THAT ARE STILL
FLOWERING AND PRO-
DUCING SATISFACTO-
RILY.

Texas and the
Gulf South

TO PROLONG THE FLOW-
ERING SEASON, CUT OFF
SPENT FLOWERS FROM
ZINNIAS, MARIGOLDS,
AND OTHER SUMMER-
BLOOMING PLANTS.

_____

_____

_____

_____

_____

_____

_____

_____

_____

_____

_____

_____

_____

_____

_____

_____

_____

_____

_____

_____

_____

_____

_____

_____

_____

Florida

AUGUST IS NORMALLY ONE OF THE HOTTEST AND RAINIEST MONTHS IN FLORIDA. WITH THE INTENSE HEAT AND HIGH HUMIDITY, OUR PLANTS TEND TO TRANSPIRE A LOT. AS A RESULT, YOU SHOULD WATER MORE FREQUENTLY AND MULCH FLOWER BEDS TO PRESERVE THE MOISTURE.

SECOND PART OF THE MONTH

SPECIAL TIPS

Mid-South

SOURWOOD, CRAPE MYRTLE, CHASTE TREES (VITEX AGNUS-CASTUS), AND SUMMER HYDRANGEA BLOOM THIS MONTH.

Texas and the Gulf South

ESTABLISH A NEW COMPOST PILE IN TIME TO INCORPORATE FALL LEAVES AND GARDEN TRIMMINGS.

Florida

There are several ways to get good watering results. Watering by hose is the most popular way because it is efficient and saves time. Invest in a top-quality reinforced rubber hose. A built-in sprinkler system, which eliminates the need for watering cans and hoses, is the most convenient method of watering. For new plantings, landscapes, and plugs, consider installing an automatic sprinkler system—your plants will appreciate it.

THIRD PART OF THE MONTH

SPECIAL TIPS

Mid-South

PRUNE, FERTILIZE AND THOROUGHLY WATER TOMATO PLANTS TO INDUCE NEW GROWTH AND A GOOD FALL FRUIT SET.

Florida

MANY PEOPLE LIKE TO SELECT SEEDS FOR FALL COLOR NOW. PETUNIAS, MARIGOLDS, AND ZINNIAS CAN ALL BE USED TO BRIGHTEN UP BEDS AND PLANTERS. YOU MAY WANT TO CHOOSE PERENNIAL COLOR SUCH AS GERANIUMS AND SHASTA AND GERBERA DAISIES. FOLKS WHO HAVE SMALL LANDSCAPE AREAS OR PLANTER BOXES AND WHO WANT SMALL PLANTS THAT STILL FLOWER SHOULD CONSIDER SWEET ALYSSUM. THIS IS A SMALL DELICATE BUSH THAT GROWS TO 8 INCHES HIGH WITH ROUNDED CLUSTERS OF FRAGRANT WHITE, LILAC, OR PURPLE BLOSSUMS. STARTED IN THE FALL, SWEET ALYSSUM MAKES AN OUTSTANDING WINTER-FLOWERING ANNUAL.

FOURTH PART OF THE MONTH

SPECIAL TIPS

Mid-South

HARVEST SEEDS OF
HOSTA AND BELACANDA
TO PLANT NEXT YEAR
FOR MANY NEW PLANTS.

Texas and the Gulf South

BE SURE TO WATER
PLANTS THAT HAVE
GREEN FRUIT OR
BERRIES. HOLLIES WILL
FREQUENTLY DROP
THEIR FRUIT WHEN
STRESSED BY DRYNESS.

Florida

THIS IS ALSO A GOOD
TIME TO CLEAR ANY
DEBRIS FROM THE GAR-
DEN PLOT AND TO TILL
AND STERILIZE THE SOIL
FOR YOUR FALL
GARDEN.

PLANT
OF THE
MONTH
AUGUST

ROSEMARY

*(Rosmarinus
officinalis)*

Many landscape plants suffer during the dry heat of August but rosemary thrives on it. Although usually cold hardy in the lower Gulf South, it may need some winter protection elsewhere. Rosemary grows well even in poor, dry rocky soils as long as the drainage is good.

The evergreen character of the narrow foliage and many horticultural forms of the plant make it quite useful. Prostrate selections are good for ground cover use or

the world, old specimens may be thinned to expose the knarled stems, creating a bonsai-like effect.

Rosemary's main appeal is its strongly scented foliage, which is popular as a fresh or dried seasoning. The fresh tops are reportedly used to distill aromatic oil used in perfumery and medicine.

Propagation is by seed or cuttings. With the renewed interest in herbs, many garden centers now stock rosemary. One-gallon size plants become established quickly. Full sun or partial shade are both good exposures. The key to successfully growing *R. officinalis* is soil with good drainage. If your soil does not drain well, try growing rosemary in a clay pot or half a whiskey barrel.

William C. Welch

to spill over retaining walls. Mature height ranges from 18 inches to 4 feet depending on the variety and growing conditions. Its small lavender-blue flowers in spring and summer are attractive but not spectacular.

Rosmarinus officinalis is a native of the Mediterranean region. Typical of many plants in that part of

---

SEPTEMBER

WHAT TO PLANT

Mid-South

September brings a change of seasons in the South. The hot sticky days of August give way to cooler, more pleasant weather and, consequently, activities in the garden change. Planting starts once again. There are many vegetables, hardy annual and perennial flowers, lawngrasses, and container-grown shrubs that can be set out this month.

Plant these vegetables from seed: beets, carrots, fall bush beans, Bibb lettuce, mustard greens, radishes, spinach, and turnips. Broccoli, cabbage, cauliflower, collard, garlic, Bibb lettuce, onion, parsley, and shallot plants and sets can all be planted now. Set plants for chrysanthemums, English daisies, pansies, hardy annuals, biennials, and perennials. For lawns, plant Kentucky 31 fescue, turf-type fescues, creeping red fescue, chewing fescue, and bluegrass.

Texas and the Gulf South

Cool-season crop transplants, such as broccoli, cauliflower, cabbage, and kale may be set out now for harvest in late fall and winter. They will need protection from the hot sun for the first 3 or 4 weeks. Strawberry plants may be set out from now through October. Poppies, cornflowers, snapdragons, calendulas, stock, sweet alyssum, larkspur, candytuft, and hollyhocks may be planted from seed or transplants from now through October and have a good chance of surviving winter in zones 8 and 9. Spring-blooming wildflower seeds, including bluebonnets, may also be sown now. Ornamental kales and cabbages are now available in many colors and forms and are excellent additions to the fall and winter garden.

Florida

It's still hurricane season here, so many gardeners won't want to plant for fear of having their seeds blown away. However, adventurous gardeners can get an early start and plant vegetables from seed.

FEEDING

Mid-South

Fertilize roses, annual flowers, tomatoes, peppers, and eggplant for a spurt of growth and more flowers and fruit. Spray chelate of iron on clorotic azaleas, camellias, and rhododendrons. Fertilize cool-season grasses with a slow-release, high-nitrogen fertilizer.

Texas and the Gulf South

Fertilize lawns with a high-nitrogen fertilizer. Be sure to water immediately after applying. An application of nitrogen fertilizer will often rejuvenate caladiums for

a few more weeks. Fertilize roses if you did not do so when you gave them a light pruning last month.

Florida

Well-fed tropical plants have been known to survive cold damage much better and recover more quickly than plants that have not received adequate nutrition. Remember, many plants still need continued watering even though the temperature has started to get cooler.

GARDEN TASKS

Mid-South

Keep vegetables picked clean to encourage more fruit. Fall apples will be ready from now through October. Pick them as they reach full color. Rake out dead crabgrass patches in cool-season lawns and reseed. Put lime on lawns this month.

Texas and the Gulf South

Divide spring-flowering perennials, such as Shasta and ox-eye daisies, irises, daylilies, cannas, violets, liriope, and ajuga. Be sure to prepare the soil well by working in organic material, such as composted pine bark, peat, or compost. About one-third of the soil in the planting area should be organic material. Prune out dead or diseased wood from trees and shrubs, but hold off on major pruning until mid-winter when they are dormant.

Florida

Prepare your vegetable garden and flower beds for the fall season. Cover the garden with 2 to 4 inches of organic matter such as compost, peat, or cow manure and till it 6 inches into the soil. Make sure to till thoroughly to incorporate the organic matter into the soil. Then sterilize the soil with Vapam.

TROUBLESHOOTING

Mid-South

Clean up insect populations on all plants before they lay their overwintering eggs. Pick scuppernongs and muscadines as they ripen to prevent bird damage.

Texas and the Gulf South

Continue a disease spray schedule for susceptible roses because black spot and mildew can be extremely damaging in September and October. Brown patch fungus can appear in September as the nights begin to cool. Look for circles of dying grass and treat with Daconil or Terraclor if any should appear.

Florida

Often during late summer and the beginning of fall, you may notice brown, dingy moths fluttering across your lawn. They are most noticeable in early morning and late afternoon. You may also see early morning moisture beads that have collected on a webbing in the grass. This indicates the presence of webworm (the moth is the mature form of the webworm). Another similar pest is army worm, which makes notches in grass blades and then eventually makes the grass appear low-cut in areas. It will look like someone has scalped your lawn with a mower. To treat both of these pests, apply Diazinon, Dursban, or Sevin.

Many people notice black soot growing on their citrus and want to know which spray will control it. The best answer is to control the insect that causes the problem. The whitefly, which is actually more closely related to scale insects than the fly, is usually the culprit. You may see little white specks when you shake the leaves. In the larvae stage, whiteflies look like hundreds of silvery white dots on the underside of the leaves. An application of Malathion or citrus spray should control them.

FIRST PART OF THE MONTH

SPECIAL TIPS

Mid-South

DO NOT PRUNE EVER-
GREENS, SPRING-FLOW-
ERING SHRUBS, AND
SPRING-FLOWERING
TREES.

YOU CAN MAKE YOUR
CHRISTMAS CACTUS
FLOWER BY SUPPLYING
IT WITH 12 HOURS OF
UNINTERRUPTED DARK-
NESS AND COOL NIGHTS
(55°F) FOR A MONTH
STARTING IN MID-OCTO-
BER. KEEP PLANTS ON
THE DRY SIDE FOR A
MONTH BEFORE BEGIN-
NING THIS TREATMENT.

Florida

If you have not pruned back those leggy poinsettias, it can still be done during the early part of this month. Don't prune them more than a few days after September 1, because trimming them too late could spoil the Christmas bloom.

SECOND PART OF THE MONTH

SPECIAL TIPS

Mid-South

MAKE CUTTINGS FROM PLANTS LIKE BEGONIA, COLEUS, GERANIUM, AND IMPATIENS. SEPTEMBER CUTTINGS ROOT EASIER THAN THOSE MADE IN OCTOBER.

Texas and the Gulf South

REJUVENATE HEAT-STRESSED GERANIUMS AND BEGONIAS FOR FALL BY LIGHTLY PRUNING, FERTILIZING, AND WATERING.

Florida

WEED YOUR BEDS, AND
TRIM BACK SHRUBS TO
THE SIZE AND SHAPE
THAT MATCHES THE
SCALE OF YOUR HOUSE.
IF SOME OF YOUR
SHRUBS HAVE BECOME
OVER-CROWDED, THIS IS
AN EXCELLENT TIME TO
REMOVE THEM.

THIRD PART OF THE MONTH

SPECIAL TIPS

Mid-South

HARVEST RIPE SEED OF ALL NON-HYBRID PLANTS THAT YOU WISH TO START DURING THE WINTER AND SPRING.

Texas and the Gulf South

PREPARE BEDS FOR SPRING-FLOWERING BULBS AS SOON AS POSSIBLE. IT IS IMPORTANT TO CULTIVATE THE SOIL AND ADD GENEROUS AMOUNTS OF ORGANIC MATTER TO IMPROVE THE DRAINAGE AND TILTH OF THE SOIL. BULBS WILL ROT WITHOUT PROPER DRAINAGE.

INTERESTED IN VINES?
VINES ARE AMONG THE
EASIEST PLANTS TO
GROW, AND WITH THEIR
MASS AND MOISTURE
CONTENT THEY CREATE
A DISTINCT COOLING
EFFECT. TO SELECT THE
RIGHT ONE FOR YOUR
NEEDS, STUDY THE
CHARACTERISTICS OF
EACH VARIETY, LEARN-
ING ABOUT THEIR
GROWTH HABITS AND
REQUIREMENTS AND
LEVELS OF RESISTANCE
TO COLD TEMPERA-
TURES. VINES ARE
CLIMBERS SO THEY
NEED SUPPORT FROM
A FENCE, TRELLIS, OR
ROUGH WALL. IF YOU DO
NOT WANT A VINE TO
SPREAD OUT OF CON-
TROL, KEEP IT TRIMMED;
THE MORE YOU TRIM A
VINE, THE BUSHIER IT
WILL BECOME. MOST
VINES HAVE TENDRILS
THAT WRAP AROUND ANY
AVAILABLE SUPPORT,
BUT SOME, SUCH AS
CLIMBING ROSES, HAVE
TO BE TIED TO A FENCE
OR TRELLIS.

FOURTH PART OF THE MONTH

SPECIAL TIPS

Mid-South

FOR A WINTER GREEN MANURE/COVER CROP, PLANT BARE VEGETABLE GARDEN AREAS WITH CRIMSON CLOVER.

Texas and the Gulf South

WHEN PLANTING SPRING-BLOOMING WILDFLOWER SEEDS, KEEP IN MIND THAT OVERSEEDING IN TURF AREAS WILL NOT PRODUCE RESULTS THAT ARE AS GOOD AS PLANT-ING IN LIGHTLY CULTI-VATED SOIL. BE SURE TO WATER WELL AFTER PLANTING.

Florida

EVERYONE WANTS TO
BE NUMBER ONE, AND
GUESS WHICH HOBBY IS
THE MOST POPULAR IN
AMERICA? GARDENING!
MANY FLORIDA GARDEN-
ERS USED TO GARDEN
IN THE NORTH, WHERE
THE SEASON IS LIMITED.
THIS IS NOT THE CASE
IN FLORIDA, WHERE
GARDENING IS A YEAR-
ROUND ACTIVITY. MAKE
SURE YOU TAKE ADVAN-
TAGE OF OUR CLIMATE
AND MAKE GARDENING
YOUR YEAR-ROUND PRO-
JECT.

PLANT OF THE MONTH

SEPTEMBER

SPIDER LILY

(Lycoris radiata)

Spider lilies are a novelty in the world of ornamental plants. Each spring the strap-shaped foliage appears, ripens, then dies down with the heat of summer. In September, usually after a soaking rain, clusters of red, pink, white, or yellow flowers suddenly spring forth from the ground. Stems may reach 18 to 24 inches and are topped with spidery-looking flowers that have wavy-edged segments and long stamens.

William C. Welch

Bulbs are best planted in July or August, although they can be moved at almost any time. *Lycoris radiata* are among the easiest perennials to grow. They thrive in full sun or partial shade and prefer to be undisturbed for several years or longer before dividing. Bulbs should be planted 3 to 4 inches deep in well-drained soil. Watering is helpful during the spring growing season and just prior to bloom in the fall. The plants need to dry out during their dormant period to bloom in the fall. We can usually count on an extended period during June, July, and August that allows for natural dormancy.

The coral-red form of *L. radiata* is by far the most common. Cream yellow and pink selections occur and are sometimes available on the trade. *L aurea* has wider leaves and larger yellow flowers. It is less cold hardy than *L. radiata*, which will naturalize throughout much of the South, and is especially well adapted to the Gulf South.

Spider lilies are most effective when naturalized and combined with ever-green ground covers such as *Vinca major, Hedera helix* (English Ivy), and *Ajuga reptans.* They are sometimes used as border or pot specimens and can go for many years before division and repotting are necessary.

Lycoris radiata provide a floral display at a time when few other plants are in bloom. This characteristic, along with a minimal water requirement and generally easy culture, make spider lilies useful and colorful additions to the southern landscape.

ACCESSORIES FOR THE GARDEN

by Dr. William C. Welch

Well-designed landscapes may need little enrichment other than the presence of people in their spaces, but since our objective is to produce the richest experience possible we often add certain details. These details may contribute little or nothing to surfacing or enclosing the garden but have a definite effect on the pleasure of our experience. For lack of a better name, we call these objects accessories. Major ones never should be afterthoughts; rather they should be planned for as the design evolves. Minor accents may be added to a completed design to give extra emphasis where necessary. All accessories within a design should be an important part of the composition.

Garden accessories are almost limitless in number; they bombard us from the pages of every popular magazine and gardening catalog. Mail order gardening catalogs now offer trellises, gazebos, arches, and arbors in a wide variety of styles and materials. Although sometimes well constructed, these items are often poorly scaled. Such structures are best designed and built as an integral part of the overall garden design and not considered as accessories.

Containers and planters are accessories that can be changed periodically. The containers themselves should be in good scale to the space as should the plants within them. Containerized plants are an opportunity for the owner to display plant collections that can add a great deal of interest and personality to the garden. Designer pottery and simple traditional clay pots are now available in many sizes, colors, and styles.

When the central well was an important utilitarian feature of the garden, necessity required that it be walled to prevent children and animals from falling in. Because its size and position made it visually important, it was only natural that people should wish to enrich its surface. In the Renaissance period, master craftsmen were employed to carve elaborate designs on their surfaces; later, ornate well heads were cast in metal. Many of these beautiful old European pieces, as well as locally produced imitations, are now to be found in formal gardens around our country. In most cases they have no utility, the well having been replaced by the city water supply. Robbed of its traditional use or even submitted to inferior uses in some cases, the well now has to be considered for its aesthetic merit alone.

A growing interest in authentic garden restoration has increased the market for antique garden accessories. Everything from gardening tools to cast iron urns, statuary, cloches (bell-like glass jars used to protect plants from the cold), and wire or wooden plant stands are increasing in value and demand along with other fine antiques. The cost of antique garden

objects has stimulated the production of many lower cost reproductions.

Sundials were the only appropriate means of telling time before watches and clocks became common. A sundial in the center of the garden became a familiar feature in Tudor gardens and is still popular today.

Bird houses and feeders are available in many styles and have become works of art that transcend their original functions. They may be considered art objects for the garden with the fringe benefits of attracting birds—who add movement, color, and seasonal interest—and providing natural insect control.

The usual mass-produced bird bath is another garden accent to be judged for its intrinsic merits and contribution to the design as a whole. Since its utility is important, it should be designed to become truly functional. Experts tell us that birds are attracted to fresh, shallow water, $1/2$ to $1^1/2$ inches deep.

Garden furniture is now being manufactured in designs that, by their formal or linear qualities, are aesthetically satisfying and appropriate for almost any situation. They are immeasurably more comfortable than the traditional cast iron bench. Formality and austerity are giving way to comfort and function. The size of garden furniture must be large to be consistent with the outdoors, yet garden furniture must be in scale with the human body. Garden furniture can be a primary source of color in a scheme. Tables, chairs, and benches can take interesting forms and be very colorful. Well-designed garden furniture will add tremendously to the richness of a landscape. They should be placed wherever they will be needed, certainly on the living terrace. Built-in furniture has the added value of remaining in place. In fact, built-in seats frequently are used as low walls for enclosing an area.

Objects not usually considered as garden accessories may actually be quite satisfactory for this purpose. Compositions can be made with driftwood, cypress knees, and weathered pieces of wood. Boulders have been used in some cases with excellent results; their rugged or smooth, water- and wind-worn surfaces seen against a complementary back-

ground of foliage, structure, or other elements create an important design effect.

Good art has elements of universal appeal and is not made less good, though it may become less valued, by whims of fashion. The problem now is one of suitability. Regardless of an element's intrinsic beauty, it is still but a fragment of the larger whole and either improves or detracts from the total effect. Designing starts with the general organization and ends with the selection of the accessories and other details.

Thus we see that the basic questions in determining whether or not to use any accessory in a garden are: (1) does it have any use; (2) is it beautiful in itself; (3) and can it be made to fit the rest of the design? Accessories, like jewels, should be used with restraint. There is no excuse for using an accessory unless it is useful *and* beautiful, and can be made to fit into the total design.

WHAT TO PLANT

Mid-South

In October, the South gets its first real taste of fall. Leaves turn and there's a briskness at night. The harvest moon comes at the end of the month along with cold nights and the danger of a killing frost throughout much of the South. By this time, dig and store sweet potatoes; harvest green tomatoes and place them on a warm, sunny window sill to ripen; take tender plants that have been outside all summer inside; make cuttings of tender perennials to carry over the winter inside; and dig bulbs and tubers that will rot in cold ground.

In the vegetable garden, plant onion sets and plants, very hardy cabbage, collards, and Austrian winter peas (for a green manure crop). In the flower garden, plant spring-flowering bulbs at the end of the month, hardy biennial and perennial roots, hardy annual plants, pansy plants, and English daisy plants. Plant Kentucky 31 fescue, turf-type fescue, and bluegrass. Overplant summer lawns with ryegrass for winter green.

Texas and the Gulf South

Now is the ideal time to divide, reset, and plant spring- and summer-flowering phlox. Among the best performing perennials for the South are *Phlox subulata*, (thrift), *Phlox pilosa* (prairie phlox),

Phlox divaricata (Louisiana phlox), and *Phlox paniculata* (summer phlox). All of these perform best when divided each year in mid-fall. Narcissus may also be planted now and in November. Select varieties that are known to naturalize in your area if perennial landscape displays are your goal. Tazetta types are generally best for the South, but many others are also good. Purchase tulips and hyacinths now but refrigerate them for 6 or more weeks (in the bottom of your refrigerator) before planting. Tall fescue grasses and ryegrass may be planted from seed this month. Sow mustard greens and turnips from seed for late fall and winter harvest.

Florida

Plant your fall vegetable garden now. Tender vegetables—tomatoes, eggplant, peppers, and squash—should be planted early. Beets, broccoli, brussel sprouts, cabbage, carrots, Swiss chard, cauliflowers, celery, lettuce, onion sets, spinach, and strawberries can all be planted, but keep an eye out for caterpillars because they like to attack them. If you do have caterpillars, treating the plants with Dipel/Thurcide will help.

This is also one of the best months to plant annual flowers such as ageratum (floss flower), sweet alyssum, begonias, calendula (also called pot marigold), candy tuft, dianthus, gerbera daisies, and the most widely used wildflower, the petunia. Petunias are often used in hanging baskets and as a bedding plant. When planting annual flowers, make sure to pick a bright, sunny spot. Also, add organic matter to the annual beds. A well-built foundation should produce a multitude of flowers.

FEEDING

Texas and the Gulf South

A light application of fertilizer can give a boost to warm-season annuals that are completing their life cycles. Holly plants with a heavy berry set often suffer from fertilizer deficiency. An application of complete fertilizer this month can be helpful now and in the spring when new growth begins.

Florida

October is an important month for the fertilization of citrus trees. Use a good citrus special at the rate of 1 pound per foot of tree spread. Fertilize trees now and they should respond in the spring with good flowering and an abundance of fruit production.

GARDEN TASKS

Mid-South

Trim and shape evergreens at the end of the month. Dig sweet potatoes and continue to harvest vegetables and apples as soon as they're ready. This is your last call to harvest seed of non-hybrid varieties. Lime lawns, unless it's already been done. Set mowers at the proper cutting height for each cool-season grass. Cut as soon as the grass reaches this height. Do not let grass grow too tall and fall over. Cut and remove all dead tops of flowers and vegetables.

Texas and the Gulf South

Prepare planting beds for pansies now so that the planting job will be easy next month. Pansies thrive in raised beds with well-prepared soil. They are also heavy feeders and appreciate frequent but light applications of nitrogen fertilizer during their growing season. If you wish to save caladium tubers for another year, dig them in late October and allow them to dry in a well-ventilated, shady area. After 7 to 10 days, remove the leaves and dirt and store them in dry peat moss, vermiculite, or similar material. Pack so that the tubers do not touch each other and dust with an all-purpose fungicide. Store the container in an area where temperatures will not drop below 50°F.

Florida

Perennials benefit greatly from mulching, which makes a flower bed more attractive, discourages weeds, inhibits soil erosion, and helps hold moisture in the soil. Cypress or pine wood chips, leaves, and grass clippings all make excellent mulches. For perennials that are dormant in winter, mulching in late October through November is recommended. Some gardeners refer to this practice as putting the perennials to bed for the winter.

The cooler season is a popular time to rescape. Most lawns and landscapes can be upgraded. Planting a bit of winter ryegrass will lend your landscape temporary green color through the fall and winter. How about putting in some new flower beds? Or consider tearing out the old, dead ligustrums and replanting with some healthy new shrubs. Something as simple as a new patio plant—like a dracaena or schefflera—will brighten up the yard. Think about undertaking an ambitious project, like building a gazebo, so you will create a new spot to enjoy our wonderful weather.

TROUBLESHOOTING

Mid-South

Pick up pecans before worms enter the nuts. Continue to pick scuppernongs and muscadines as they ripen to prevent bird damage. Rake leaves off lawns before they mat and damage grasses. Keep leaves from piling around the stems of shrubs, especially azaleas, camellias, and other broadleaf evergreens. Continue to clean up insect populations on all plants before they lay their overwintering eggs. Control any infestations of scale.

Texas and the Gulf South

Continue to watch for brown patch fungus in St. Augustine lawns. Terraclor or Daconil will usually stop the spread, but the damaged grass will have little chance for recovery before next spring.

FIRST PART OF THE MONTH

SPECIAL TIPS

Mid-South

DIG SWEET POTATOES
WHEN THERE ARE HEAVY
RADIAL CRACKS AT THE
MAIN STEM.

Texas and the Gulf South

IF YOUR TREES,
SHRUBS, OR ROSES ARE
DROPPING MANY TWIGS
AND BRANCHES, THEY
MAY HAVE BEEN INFECT-
ED BY TWIG GIRDLERS.
MAKE SURE ALL THE
TWIGS AND BRANCHES
THAT DROP ARE
DESTROYED BECAUSE
THAT'S WHERE THE TWIG
GIRDLERS DEPOSIT
THEIR EGGS.

_____
_____
_____
_____
_____
_____
_____
_____
_____
_____
_____
_____
_____
_____
_____
_____
_____
_____
_____
_____
_____
_____
_____

Florida

IN THE FALL MONTHS YOU WILL FIND A GOOD SELECTION OF ROSES AND OTHER FLOWERS. ROSES MUST HAVE NO LESS THAN 6 HOURS OF DIRECT SUN TO REACH THEIR FLOWERING POTENTIAL. ROSE BEDS SHOULD HAVE GOOD DRAINAGE AND A WATER SOURCE, SUCH AS A GARDEN HOSE, NEARBY.

SECOND PART OF THE MONTH

SPECIAL TIPS

Mid-South

DIG CALADIUM AND ELE-
PHANT'S EAR TUBERS
BEFORE A KILLING
FROST.

START COLLECTING
LEAVES FOR COMPOST-
ING. BE SURE TO HAVE
ENOUGH SOIL TO COVER
EACH 6-INCH LAYER OF
LEAVES WITH SEVERAL
INCHES OF SOIL. ADD
ABOUT 1 POUND OF A
COMPLETE LAWN OR
GARDEN FERTILIZER TO
EACH LEAF LAYER TO
PROVIDE THE NECES-
SARY NITROGEN FOR
DECOMPOSITION (COM-
POSTED MANURE MAY
ALSO BE USED). THOR-
OUGHLY WET THE LEAF
LAYER BEFORE ADDING
SOIL.

_____

_____

_____

_____

_____

_____

_____

_____

_____

_____

_____

_____

_____

_____

_____

_____

_____

_____

_____

_____

_____

_____

_____

JUST BECAUSE PERENNIAL BEDS ARE EASIER TO CARE FOR DOESN'T MEAN THEY DON'T HAVE TO BE PLANNED CAREFULLY. PERENNIALS, AS A RULE, SHOULD BE PLANTED IN WELL-DRAINED AREAS. IF YOUR LANDSCAPE DOESN'T HAVE OPTIMUM DRAINAGE CONDITIONS, IT'S A GOOD IDEA TO PLANT YOUR PERENNIALS IN RAISED BEDS, WHICH IMPROVES DRAINAGE AND DELINEATES LANDSCAPE AREAS. A RAISED BED CAN BE BUILT BY CREATING A SQUARE RECTANGLE WITH RAILROAD TIES, LOGS, OR PRESSURE-TREATED LUMBER. COMPLETELY FILL THE CENTER AREA WITH A QUALITY POTTING SOIL AND YOUR BED IS FINISHED.

THIRD PART OF THE MONTH

SPECIAL TIPS

Mid-South

PRIZED GERANIUMS MAY BE DUG AND STORED OVER THE WINTER. DIG THE PLANTS AND LEAVE SOME DIRT AROUND THE ROOTS. WRAP THE ROOTS IN A PLASTIC BAG, LEAVING THE TOPS OUT. LAY THEM ON THEIR SIDES IN A LIGHT, COOL PLACE WHERE THEY WON'T FREEZE.

IF YOU HAVE SAVED SEEDS FROM YOUR FAVORITE PLANTS, AIR DRY THEM FIRST AND THEN PLACE THEM IN AN AIRTIGHT CONTAINER AND REFRIGERATE. CAREFULLY LABEL EACH PACKET. REMEMBER, PLANTS GROWN FROM HYBRID PLANT SEED OFTEN DIFFER CONSIDERABLY FROM THE PARENT PLANT.

_____

_____

_____

_____

_____

_____

_____

_____

_____

_____

_____

_____

_____

_____

_____

_____

_____

_____

_____

_____

_____

_____

MANY GARDENERS DIVIDE THEIR LANDSCAPES INTO SPECIFIC AREAS: SOME AREAS FOR PERENNIALS THAT BECOME PERMANENT PARTS OF THE GARDEN'S LAYOUT AND OTHER AREAS FOR ANNUALS, WHICH MAY BE CHANGED AT THE GROWER'S WHIM. PERENNIALS, HOWEVER, SHOULD BE LEFT WHERE THEY ARE PLANTED INITIALLY SO THEY CAN GROW AND MATURE WITHOUT INTERRUPTION, AS DO TREES AND SHRUBS. RELOCATING ANY PLANT WILL SET IT BACK AND INHIBIT ITS OVERALL GROWTH AND FLOWERING CAPABILITIES.

FOURTH PART OF THE MONTH

_____

_____

_____

_____

_____

_____

SPECIAL TIPS

_____

START PAPERWHITE NAR-
CISSUS INSIDE AT THE
END OF THE MONTH FOR
BLOSSOMS IN EARLY
DECEMBER. KEEP THE
WATER LEVEL BELOW THE
BOTTOM OF THE BULB
AFTER THE ROOTS HAVE
EXTENDED MORE THAN
AN INCH. THIS WILL
KEEP BULBS FROM
SPEWING UP IN THE
BOWL. AFTER THE
SHOOTS ARE 4 OR 5
INCHES TALL, PLACE
THE BOWLS IN A BRIGHT
SPOT TO KEEP THE
PLANTS STOCKY.

_____

_____

_____

_____

_____

_____

_____

_____

_____

_____

_____

Texas and the Gulf South

_____

REMOVE DAMAGED OR
DEAD LIMBS FROM YOUR
SHADE AND FRUIT TREES
BEFORE THEY DROP
THEIR FOLIAGE. IT IS
MUCH EASIER TO DETER-
MINE WHICH LIMBS ARE
ALIVE WHEN THEY STILL
HAVE THEIR GREEN
FOLIAGE.

_____

_____

_____

_____

_____

_____

A Southern Gardener's Notebook

Florida

WATERING IS CRUCIAL
TO YOUR PERENNIALS'
CONTINUED GOOD
HEALTH. MOST NEED A
GOOD WEEKLY DOSE.
GIVE THEM $^1/_2$ INCH OF
WATER TWICE A WEEK
TO ENSURE THAT THEIR
THIRST IS ADEQUATELY
QUENCHED.

PLANT OF THE MONTH

OCTOBER

FIREBUSH

(Hamelia patens)

Actually a large shrub or small tree native to Mexico, firebush is a dependable and useful perennial for the southern half of the South. It freezes to the ground and resprouts each spring, typically producing a 4- to 5-foot mound of reddish orange flowers from early summer until late fall.

In addition to its long blooming season, the plant has several other significant attributes. *Hamelia* is very drought tolerant and thrives in most any soil as long as it is well drained. Full sun or partially shaded locations are preferable to shady ones, which will result in rank growth and little bloom. The foliage often turns bright red before freezing back and the small, dark fruit is edible. In Mexico, a fermented drink is said to be made from the fruit. The leaves and stems have been used for tanning and a concoction from the leaves is reportedly used for various medicinal purposes.

The flower buds last longer than the flowers themselves and appear in great numbers. After maturing, the flowers drop off quickly and the plant requires only occasional shearing to keep it in a nearly perpetual state of bloom.

Dr. Jerry Parsons

NOVEMBER

WHAT TO PLANT

Mid-South

Killing frosts and hard freezes throughout the region end this year's growing season for southern gardeners. But now there is a new one—the dormant planting season. Just ahead is the time to plant all types of trees, shrubs, and fruits.

The following may now be planted: balled-and-burlapped and container-grown evergreen trees and shrubs; balled-and-burlapped, container-grown, and bare-root deciduous shrubs and trees; container-grown, bare-root, and packaged fruits; and bare-root and packaged roses. In the flower garden, plant spring-flowering bulbs, hardy biennial and perennial roots, pansy plants, and English daisy plants. For lawns, plant Kentucky 31 fescue, turf-type fescue, and bluegrass at the beginning of the month. Overplant summer lawns with ryegrass so you'll have winter green color early in the month.

Texas and the Gulf South

November is the best time to plant pansies and their cousins, violas. By planting now, the first blooms should appear before Christmas. Pansies and violas flower sporadically during the winter while the plants are growing, and then create a wonderful display when warmer weather comes. Look for new colors, sizes, and forms that may be available. All pansies and violas like to be in a sunny location and to have well-prepared and well-drained soil. This usually means you will have to raise the planting bed at least 4 to 6 inches above the surrounding area and incorporate organic material in the form of composted pine bark, peat, or your own compost. When finished, the mixture in your bed should be at least one-third organic material. Flowering kale and cabbage are also available in a variety of leaf shapes and colors. Small patches of turnips, spinach, and mustard greens can be sown periodically to stagger harvest over a longer period. Plant daffodils, oxalis, Dutch irises, ipheion, and leucojum now for spring bloom but keep tulips and hyacinths in the lower part of your refrigerator until late December or early January. Select and plant camellias and sasanquas now while you can see them in bloom. Complete seeding ryegrass and fescue this month.

Florida

Now is the time to plant winter ryegrass. To ensure best germination conditions, rake the ground lightly, apply the seed, and rake lightly afterwards. The recommended amount of ryegrass seed is between 5 and 15 pounds per 1000 square feet of lawn. Water the grass twice daily until the seed germinates, and then only a couple of times a week once it is well established. Remember, this is such a fast-growing grass that you will have to fertilize and mow throughout fall and winter.

English snap peas like our coolest season, so it's an excellent time to plant these hardy vegetables.

FEEDING

Mid-South, Texas, and the Gulf South

Reduce the rate and frequency of fertilizer applications for houseplants from now until March because plants do not need the food, and may actually be harmed by it in the winter when their growth rates are naturally slower. Continue to fertilize winter annuals and perennials. Apply high-nitrogen fertilizer to ryegrass and fescue plantings.

Florida

If you planted vegetables in October, make sure that you are fertilizing them on a regular basis. Give them a nourishing plant food once a week.

GARDEN TASKS

Mid-South

Finish harvesting all vegetables still standing in the garden. Pick Japanese persimmons as soon as they begin to soften. Mow cool-season grasses regularly to encourage plant development. Again, cut and remove all dead tops of flowers and vegetables and keep leaves from collecting around trees' and shrubs' stems. Prune back roses about one-third.

Texas and the Gulf South

Power lawn equipment will start and run better next spring if you drain the gasoline and run the engine until it stops. Drain and store hoses and other portable irrigation equipment, but keep them handy in the event you need them this winter.

Florida

Many root-crop vegetables, such as carrots, radishes, beets, and turnips will need to be thinned now. This will give the young plants more room to grow; most of them need to be 4 to 6 inches apart to develop properly.

Fall is a great time to set trees into the landscape. As the nights grow cooler, newly installed trees suffer less of a shock than when planted in warmer months. You may want to have a nursery expert or a landscaper plant the trees. If you plant them yourself, remember to plant them at the same depth they were set at in the container. Dig the hole twice as wide as the rootball and plant the tree upright in the center of the hole. In many cases, you may want to enrich the planting hole by adding peat moss and cow manure before filling it.

TROUBLESHOOTING

Mid-South

Continue to rake leaves off lawns so they don't mat and damage grasses. Watch for scale infestation and control immediately if a problem develops.

Texas and the Gulf South

Continue to watch for brown patch fungus in St. Augustine turf and treat with Terraclor or Daconil as needed. The first frost of the season occurs in most of the South this month. Be prepared to protect plants, including fall tomatoes. Protecting once or twice can extend the production of vine-ripened tomatoes and peppers a month or more.

Florida

November is usually a dry month, and because of this, spider mites may attack citrus and junipers. To control mites, spray with Kelthane and respray within 5 days to kill the second generation.

FIRST PART OF THE MONTH

SPECIAL TIPS

IF YOU WANT PAPER-WHITE NARCISSUS BLOSSOMS FOR CHRISTMAS, START THEM NOW. REMEMBER TO KEEP THE WATER LEVEL BELOW THE BOTTOM OF THE BULBS AFTER THE ROOTS HAVE EXTENDED MORE THAN AN INCH. WHEN SHOOTS ARE 4 OR 5 INCHES TALL, PLACE THE BOWLS IN A BRIGHT SPOT.

Texas and the Gulf South

SHAPE AND PRUNE CONTAINER PLANTS BEFORE BRINGING THEM INDOORS OR INTO THE GREENHOUSE FOR THE WINTER.

_____

_____

_____

_____

_____

_____

_____

_____

_____

_____

_____

_____

_____

_____

_____

_____

_____

_____

_____

_____

_____

_____

_____

_____

UNIVERSITY RESEARCH HAS SHOWN THAT POINSETTIAS ARE NOT POISONOUS UNLESS AN INDIVIDUAL HAS AN ALLERGY TO THEM—SO PLACE THESE BEAUTIFUL, LONG-LASTING PLANTS AROUND YOUR HOME AND ENJOY THEM.

SECOND PART OF THE MONTH

SPECIAL TIPS

Don't forget to gather pecans as soon as they fall from the trees.

Pill bugs, slugs, and snails like your pansies almost as much as you do. They can be devastating when the plants are small. To control them, use commercial bug baits or, for slugs, place jar lids filled with beer among the plants.

_____
_____
_____
_____
_____
_____
_____
_____
_____
_____
_____
_____
_____
_____
_____
_____
_____
_____
_____
_____
_____
_____
_____
_____
_____
_____

A Southern Gardener's Notebook

Florida

It's not too early to think about cold protection. Planning now may make the difference when the temperatures suddenly drop. Some of the plants you should protect are: bananas, bougainvillea, poinsettias, copper leaf, ixora, schefflera, allamandas, papaya, and all tropical trees. Start saving boxes that could be placed over plants and begin collecting burlap to cover bedding plants.

THIRD PART OF THE MONTH

SPECIAL TIPS

STARTING WITH THANKS-GIVING, HOLIDAY FLOW-ERING PLANTS, LIKE AZALEAS, CHRYSANTHE-MUMS, HYDRANGEAS, AND POINSETTIAS, WILL BRIGHTEN HOMES. THESE PLANTS ALL HAVE SPECIFIC REQUIREMENTS FOR EXISTING INDOORS WHERE FURNACES DRY THE ATMOSPHERE AND SHORT WINTER DAYS MAKE HOMES DARK INSIDE. BECAUSE OF THIS, YOUR HOLIDAY PLANTS WILL NEED HELP TO STAY BEAUTIFUL THROUGH THE SEASON. THEY SHOULD BE MIST-ED FREQUENTLY WITH FRESH WATER TO KEEP FLOWERS HEALTHY. KEEP THE SOIL DAMP BUT DO NOT OVER-WATER.

Texas and the Gulf South

Check patio and hanging container plants for mealy bugs, spider mites, and scale before taking them into the house or greenhouse for the winter. To treat, apply an insecticidal soap or any other material labeled for this use.

Florida

Aphids, scale, mites, and grasshoppers are just a few of the pests that can be a problem. In the North, mole crickets, chinch bugs, and fruit flies give gardeners trouble. Most of these pests can be controlled with a general insecticide like Malathion or Diazinon. Use caution and follow the directions on the label whenever you apply insecticide. Many gardeners think that if 2 teaspoons are a good dose, then 4 teaspoons must work even better. Don't make this big mistake!

FOURTH PART OF THE MONTH

SPECIAL TIPS

CLEAN UP SHOULD CONTINUE AS THE LAST LEAVES FALL FROM DECIDUOUS TREES AND FREEZING TEMPERATURES KILL THE LAST FLOWER AND VEGETABLE TOPS. REMEMBER HOW VALUABLE THESE MATERIALS CAN BE WHEN COMPOSTED AND USED AS ORGANIC MATTER DURING SOIL PREPARATION NEXT YEAR.

TREES AND SHRUBS WITH COLORFUL BERRIES WILL HOLD THEIR FRUIT MUCH LONGER IF THEY HAVE ADEQUATE MOISTURE AVAILABLE.

There are three kinds of pest control you are most likely to use: contact poison, systemic insecticides, and stomach poisons. Malathion and Diazinon are contact poisons because they kill on contact. Dimethoate, Cygon, and Orthene are considered systemic insecticides because they are absorbed into the plant and then consumed by the plant eater, killing it when the poison enters its blood stream. Sevin and Dipel are stomach poisons that effectively kill chewing caterpillars. The caterpillars die when they chew on the plant, ingest the poison, and absorb it through their stomach walls. These poisons are popular because they don't kill beneficial bugs and can be applied to a plant the same day its produce is harvested.

PLANT OF THE MONTH

NOVEMBER

Greg Grant

POSSUM-HAW HOLLY

(Ilex Decidua)

Each year in November there is a flurry of interest in the Yaupon-like plant without any leaves. Actually, the foliage of *Ilex decidua* can last into late December but eventually drops, leaving a spectacular show of red, orange, or, occasionally, yellow fruit on the female plant. The berries usually remain all winter or until removed by the cedar waxwing or one of the other nine species known to feed on the fruit.

Possum-haws are useful in the landscape as large shrubs or small trees and may occur with single or multiple trunks. Female plants are preferable because the males have little ornamental value.

Culture is easy. Possum-haws are native from West Texas to well into the eastern part of the South and grow in a wide variety of soil and moisture conditions. They tolerate poor drainage quite well, but will also thrive under fairly dry situations.

Availability is getting better but expect some difficulty in locating nursery-grown plants. Some nurseries are now growing female selections from cuttings, which assures the fruit color and sex of the plant. Seed are easily propagated but result in a high percentage of male plants. Determining their gender is not practical until plants are old enough to flower, which may be 2 to 4 years later.

If you collect specimens from their native habitats (get permission first), keep two things in mind. First, select a plant with at least a few berries and second, unless you have access to large-scale digging equipment, choose a small plant. Possum-haws grow quickly once established, but plants that are large when collected can be slow to recover from transplanting.

DECEMBER

WHAT TO PLANT

Mid-South

The last month of the year is a happy time for southern gardeners. Flower beds and vegetable gardens are finished for the season. Fruits have been harvested, lawns planted or rejuvenated, and spring bulbs planted. It is time to relish what has been and to start planning for next year. There is plenty of inspiration because *Camellia sasanquas* and the more spectacular *Camellia japonicas* are flowering, which proves that southern gardens never sleep. Seed and nursery catalogs arrive with the newest varieties as well as old favorites. It is easy to sit by the fire and dream of the beautiful flowers and delicious home-grown vegetables that next season will bring.

Continue dormant-season plantings. Plant balled-and-burlapped and container-grown evergreen trees and shrubs; balled-and-burlapped, container-grown, and bare-root deciduous shrubs, vines, and trees; container-grown, bare-root, and packaged fruits; and bare-root and packaged roses. Spring-flowering bulbs may still be planted until the end of the month. Also plant hardy biennial and perennial roots.

Texas and the Gulf South

Continue planting pansies, calendulas, violas, stock, snapdragons, and pinks from transplants. Larkspur, poppies, and cornflowers may still be planted from seed the first part of the month. Narcissus can also be planted in December. Remove tulips and hyacinths from refrigeration and plant by the end of the month, if possible. Plant old-fashioned vining nasturtiums from seed in your greenhouse so you will have interesting and fragrant cut flowers in late winter.

Florida

Easter lilies planted in December will normally bloom from mid-March through April. You might also dig up a bed of amaryllis or crinum lilies and replant them. Add extra peat and dehydrated cow manure to the bulb beds and you will be rewarded with many flowers in the spring.

FEEDING

Mid-South, Texas and the Gulf South

Apply water-soluble fertilizer to pansies and other cool-season annuals and perennials you have just set out. Use little, if any fertilizer on houseplants and tropicals you have brought indoors for the winter. Apply small amounts of nitrogen to broccoli, collards, turnips, and mustard greens.

Florida

If you have a vegetable garden, remember most of our vegetables are annuals. This means you must either fertilize them with a water-soluble plant food weekly, or with a 6-6-6 sidedress every 3 to 4 weeks. (Sidedressing means to apply the fertilizer about 8 inches from the stems or trunks of the vegetables.)

GARDEN TASKS

Mid-South

Continue raking those pesky oak leaves, and any other leaves that may have fallen on your lawn. If you didn't prune your roses in November, prune them back one-third now. Start pruning fruits after several hard freezes. Shade trees may now be pruned, but never top them.

Texas and the Gulf South

Dig holes or prepare beds for roses you will be receiving in the mail or buying from garden centers in January or February. Whether your soil is mostly sand or clay, organic material, such as composted pine bark, compost, or peat with existing soil and a small amount of balanced fertilizer. One-half to one-third of the mixture should be organic material. The mixture should be mellow and easily removed when planting time arrives. Prune grapes soon after they become dormant. Peaches, plums, apples, and other fruit trees may be pruned from now until late winter.

Florida

This is an important month for pruning. Apples and peaches should be trimmed into the modified leader system, which means leaving the main branches and thinning out branches that are growing toward the tree's center. This allows light to reach the center of the tree, increasing its growth and production in the spring. If sunlight does not reach the tree's center, all of the fruit will set on the perimeter of the tree. Grapes should be trimmed back to the main runner. It is also best to trim oaks and maples during the dormant season.

Major rose trimming should be done in late December or early January. Normally, roses are trimmed back one-half to one-third so that the new growth is removed. Most citrus should be trimmed when necessary—sometimes you may find a scraggly branch growing out of bounds that needs trimming. Be careful not to trim hedges too severely.

TROUBLESHOOTING

Mid-South

Control any scale infestations. Start dormant spraying of fruits and roses at the end of the month.

Texas and the Gulf South

Look for scale insects on trees and shrubs and apply dormant oil spray as needed. Dormant oil is an excellent preventative spray for fruit and pecan trees.

Florida

When foliage plants are moved into a home or office for the winter, they need time to become adjusted to the drier and darker conditions. If they don't have enough adjustment time, their leaves may turn yellow and they may drop their foliage. These plants will also have a difficult time recovering from the move if they do not have enough light—they cannot photosynthesize (make food) without the proper light level. Make sure foliage plants are placed a few feet from a bright window. If they are placed on a window ledge, rotate their pots occasionally to encourage equal growth on all sides.

William D. Adams

FIRST
PART
OF THE
MONTH

SPECIAL TIPS

Mid-South

KEEP LEAVES AND
OTHER PLANT TRASH
FROM COLLECTING
AROUND THE LOWER
STEMS OF SHRUBS,
ESPECIALLY AZALEAS,
BOXWOOD, ELAEAGNUS,
AND HOLLIES. THE
VOLE, A SHORT-TAILED
MOUSELIKE CREATURE,
OFTEN HIDES IN THE
MULCH WHILE CHEWING
THE BARK OFF THESE
PLANTS.

Texas and the Gulf South

REPLENISH MULCH AROUND TREES AND SHRUBS TO INSULATE THEM FROM THE COLD AND TO HELP THEM RETAIN MOISTURE DURING THE WINTER. REMEMBER, PLANTS DON'T ONLY SUFFER FROM MOISTURE STRESS IN THE SUMMER—WINTER'S NORTHERN WINDS CAN DRY OUT THEIR ROOTS AND CAUSE SIGNIFICANT DAMAGE.

Florida

BEGIN THINKING ABOUT A COLD PROTECTION PLAN. WE NORMALLY EXPERIENCE OUR FIRST FREEZE BY DECEMBER 15. PLANNING NOW MAY MAKE THE DIFFERENCE BETWEEN KEEPING A TROPICAL ALIVE AND LOSING IT. SOME OF THE MORE DELICATE TROPICAL PLANTS WILL USUALLY FARE BETTER ON THE SOUTH SIDE OF YOUR HOME. MULCHING THE GROUND CAN ALSO HELP BY INCREASING THE TEMPERATURE OF THE GROUND BY AS MUCH AS 2 TO 3 DEGREES.

SECOND PART OF THE MONTH

SPECIAL TIPS

FERTILIZER IS NOT FOOD FOR PLANTS, DESPITE THE CLAIMS ON MANY BAGS OF GARDEN FERTILIZER THAT THEY ARE COMPLETE "PLANT FOODS." THE MINERALS IN FERTILIZER—NITROGEN, PHOSPHOROUS, AND POTASH—ARE NECESSARY FOR PLANT GROWTH, BUT THEY DO NOT FEED THE PLANT. THEY ARE MERELY ABSORBED INTO THE PLANT, WHERE THEY PROVIDE THE ELEMENTS FOR GROWTH TO TAKE PLACE.

SELECT GARDENING BOOKS, TOOLS, AND PLANTS FOR FRIENDS WHO ARE ALSO GARDENING ENTHUSIASTS.

Many plants work as holiday decorations and Christmas cactus is one of them. Continue watering it, but make sure it doesn't get too wet. Try to keep it away from heating ducts, because direct drafts can make it drop its flower buds. Of course, poinsettias are also wonderful holiday plants. As you may know, they are usually admired for their flowers, which are actually bracts, or modified leaves. Your poinsettia may need to be sprayed for caterpillars with an organic material called Thuricide/Dipel.

THIRD
PART
OF THE
MONTH

SPECIAL TIPS

Texas and the Gulf South

REMEMBER TO WATER EVERGREEN PLANTS THAT MAY BE PROTECTED BY ROOF OVERHANGS DURING THE WINTER MONTHS.

_____
_____
_____
_____
_____
_____
_____
_____
_____
_____
_____
_____
_____
_____
_____
_____
_____
_____
_____
_____
_____
_____
_____

To prolong the life of your Christmas tree, fill the stand's liquid holder with the following solution:

1 gallon hot water

$1/4$ cup iron chelate

2 cups light corn syrup

4 teaspoons chlorine bleach

To make your tree more fire resistant, mist it thoroughly with the following solution:

9 ounces Borax

4 ounces boric acid crystals or powder

1 gallon warm water

FOURTH PART OF THE MONTH

SPECIAL TIPS

THE GENERAL RULE FOR BULB PLANTING DEPTH IS TO PLANT THREE TIMES THE GREATEST DIAMETER OF THE BULB FOR LARGE BULBS AND FOUR TIMES FOR SMALL BULBS.

Texas and the Gulf South

REMOVE LARGE ACCUMULATIONS OF LEAVES FROM TURF AREAS AND ADD THEM TO THE COMPOST PILE.

_____
_____
_____
_____
_____
_____
_____
_____
_____
_____
_____
_____
_____
_____
_____
_____
_____
_____
_____
_____
_____
_____
_____
_____
_____
_____

Florida

IF YOUR GARDEN IS DAMAGED BY THE COLD, DO NOT TRIM OFF DAMAGED BRANCHES UNTIL MARCH OR APRIL WHEN THE DANGER OF ADDITIONAL FROSTS HAS PASSED. SOME GARDENERS GET OUT THEIR PRUNING SHEARS THE DAY AFTER A FREEZE, BUT TRIMMING ENTICES A PLANT TO PRODUCE NEW GROWTH THAT MAY BE KILLED BY ANOTHER COLD SPELL. ALSO LEAVE DEAD LEAVES AND BRANCHES ALONE—THEY PROVIDE SOME PROTECTION UNTIL THE WARM WEATHER ARRIVES. IT IS SAFE TO TREAT FOR COLD DAMAGE ONCE PLANTS BEGIN TO SPROUT. STARTING AT THE END OF A DAMAGED BRANCH, TRIM UNTIL YOU REACH FRESH, HEALTHY GROWTH. ALWAYS PAINT THE NEWLY CUT END OF A BRANCH WITH NEUTRAL COPPER AND PRUNING PAINT TO PROTECT AGAINST INFECTION AND EXCESSIVE SAP DRAINAGE.

PLANT OF THE MONTH

DECEMBER

GARDEN VIOLET

(Viola odorata)

William C. Welch

Violets were once considered indispensable perennials for the well-designed garden. Although numerous native voilet species occur in the South, the violet of choice for most southern gardens is *V. odorata*, which is of European, Asian, and African origin. Dark blue or purple is the predominant color. Well into the early twentieth century, violets were among the most popular florist-cut flowers. Their fragrance, rich colors, and relatively easy culture made them popular nationwide.

Violets prefer a rich, moist but well-drained soil high in organic content. They also do best in partially shaded locations. Their natural bloom period is late winter and early spring.

Although evergreen, garden violets become semidormant during our long, hot summers. They can, however, endure considerable drought and heat stress and usually become lush and healthy with the onset of cooler and more moist fall and winter conditions.

Landscape uses include borders and ground covers. Large container shrubs can often be enhanced by a mass of violets at their base, providing attractive foliage, fragrance, and color at a season when few other plants are at their peak. Mature height is usually 8 to 10 inches. The rounded foliage is quite attractive even when the plants are not in bloom.

Propagation is usually done by dividing mature clumps during early to mid-fall. Seeds can also be used to produce new plants but require considerable attention during the early stages.

Garden violet borders may still be found in some of the old gardens of the South. They can be long-living, relatively low-maintenance perennials. Few plants perform as well in shady areas and offer color and fragrance during January, February, and March.

A Southern Gardener's Notebook

NOTES

TREE AND SHRUB NOTES

Use this page to record the progress of your trees and shrubs. For example, when they were planted, growth, problems, and pruning schedules are some of the records you might keep.

FRUIT TREE NOTES

Fruit trees obviously have special needs. You might keep a journal of spray schedules, pest or disease problems, whether your tree is self-pollinated, and fruit quality.

PERENNIAL NOTES

With most perennials—especially those in a perennial border—it will be helpful to track their progress through the seasons, so that you can successfully "pull together" the garden at any time of the year.

HERB NOTES

Herbs are increasingly popular parts of the garden, both for their practical/culinary uses and for their aesthetic impact. And they are some of the most care-free plants you'll find, most tolerating poor soils as long as they have good drainage.

VEGETABLE NOTES

Whether you have simply a container of tomato plants or have given your whole yard over to the vegetable garden, it will be helpful to note feeding and watering schedules, pest and disease problems, days to maturity, when planted, success of harvest, etc.

PEST AND DISEASE NOTES

Although we've discussed in our "Troubleshooting" sections what to look for and how to "fix" it, you will probably have your own very special set of circumstances. Frequently examine your plants so that you can nip any problem in the bud (so to speak).

WEATHER NOTES

The map at the beginning of the Notebook *will give you a general idea of what's going on in your region, but it's helpful to consider also your microclimate, the climate of a very specific space that is influenced by geography, local development, etc.*

SOIL NOTES

As we've previously mentioned, a soil test is an important part of getting your garden started—or of improving the garden you have. Keep notes of soil tests and the amendments you make.

PHOTOGRAPHY CREDITS

Title page: Anemones, William D. Adams.
Copyright page: Bench with *Gladiolus byzantinus*, William C. Welch.
Page 6: The perennial garden, William C. Welch.
Page 22: Cabbage, calendula, and lobelia at Calloway Gardens, Georgia, Jerry Pavia.
Page 33: Flowering quince, William D. Adams.
Page 34: Paperwhites, William D. Adams.
Page 46: Winter honeysuckle, William C. Welch.
Page 48: Tulips and azaleas, William D. Adams.
Page 59: Louisiana iris, William C. Welch.
Page 64: Flowering dogwood and azaleas, Georgia, Jerry Pavia.
Page 76: Nasturtium, William C. Welch.
Page 78: Clematis, William D. Adams.
Page 89: Yarrow, William C. Welch.
Page 90: 'Olympic' lilies, William D. Adams.
Page 101: Larkspur, William C. Welch.
Page 104: 'Climbing Cécile Brünner' and shasta daisies, William C. Welch.
Page 106: `Betty Prior' rose, nicotiana, lamb's ear, and sweet william, Georgia, Joanne Pavia.
Page 118: Giant rose mallow, William C. Welch.
Page 120: Coleus, William D. Adams.
Page 130: Rosemary, William C. Welch.
Page 132: Mexican bush sage, Dallas Arboretum, Carolyn Brown.
Page 142: Spider lily, William C. Welch.
Page 144: Garden accessories, William C. Welch.
Page 146: 'Rococo' pansy, William D. Adams.
Page 158: Firebush, Dr. Jerry Parsons.
Page 160: 'Grandchild' mums, William D. Adams.
Page 170: Possum-haw holly, Greg Grant.
Page 172: The last leaf, William D. Adams.
Page 182: Violet, William C. Welch.

The Littlest Snowman

Story by CHARLES TAZEWELL

Pictures by GEORGE DE SANTIS

GROSSET & DUNLAP • NEW YORK

Library of Congress Catalog Card Number: 67-23811
1970 Printing
Originally published in December, 1955 *Coronet* Magazine.
© 1955, 1956 by Charles Tazewell.
Illustrations © 1958, by Wonder Books, a Division of Grosset & Dunlap, Inc.
All rights reserved under International and Pan-American Copyright Conventions.
Published simultaneously in Canada.   Printed in the United States of America.

In a certain town, on a certain first of December morning, everyone was suddenly awakened from his Christmas dreams by the joyful ringing of bells in every tower and steeple.

When the townspeople looked out of their windows, they saw a white carpet of snow all over the ground. Every street lamp wore a white robe and every picket on every fence wore a funny little snowcap. And rolling down the snowy street, behind two hard-working men who were clearing a path with their shovels, was a long convertible being driven by His Honor, the Mayor!

There was no doubt about it now — it was time for the birth of the Littlest Snowman! The people dashed out of their houses, following the Mayor's car to a house which stood on Winter Avenue.

There, in a yard, they saw a small boy — the only one in town who knew how to make the Littlest Snowman. He was just patting the last bit of snow into place. Around him were many helpers. Grandfather Squirrel held the Littlest Snowman's old brown hat. Reuben Rabbit had the red handle of a broken kitchen spoon which would soon be the Littlest Snowman's mouth. Mr. and Mrs. English Sparrow carried two pieces of coal for the eyes. And Marmaduke Mouse had a blue marble which would be the nose. Most important of all was a candy heart on which was lettered "I Love You Truly," held by the little golden-haired girl from next door.

As soon as the Littlest Snowman's heart was pressed gently into place beneath the second bottle-top button of his vest, the Mayor made his speech of welcome. Then the crowd paraded to the park in the center of town. There the Biggest Christmas Tree to be found in the Fir Forest of the Far North was decorated with thousands of ornaments and glittering tinsel. The Littlest Snowman pressed a switch and the Biggest Christmas Tree was instantly lighted by many colored lights.

Then the Weather Man stepped forward. He was as long and as thin as the glass on a thermometer and on his tall silk hat was a weather vane. On the end of a watch chain across his vest was a turnip-sized barometer. "I predict," he said, "that it will start to snow again on Christmas Eve, and that we will have an old-fashioned White Christmas this year!"

Everyone agreed that this was the best forecast the Weather Man had ever made.

Some evenings later, when the stars were twinkling brightly, the Littlest Snowman received a special-delivery letter by helicop-pigeon inviting him to attend the annual Snowmen's Snow Ball at Town Park.

The famous Snow Ball was already well under way when the Littlest Snowman arrived. He lost no time in joining the Snowladies and Snowgentlemen who were waltzing gracefully to the sleighbell music. Then, when he had had enough of dancing, he helped himself to some ice water from the punch bowl on the refreshment table and also to some appetizing colored icicles.

Suddenly, over the music and voices of the dancers, a scream was heard from one of the Snowgirls. "Look at the Snake!" she shrieked.

All the Snowpeople turned and stared at the large thermometer which hung on a tree. Snake, in Snowpeople language, meant the long red line which went up and down on the thermometer.

"The Snake is crawling up and up!" squealed the Snowgirl again.

And it was! The Snake was already wiggling well above the freezing mark.

"I'm melting!" wailed a fat Snowlady.

"I'm defrosting!" cried a Snowman.

"Hurry!" someone shouted. "Let's go back to our yards and pull the snow blankets over our heads." With each fat little foot leaving a puddle of water behind him, the Littlest Snowman slushed homeward sadly.

For the next few weeks, the red Snake in the thermometer never crawled down below the freezing mark, and the Littlest Snowman became thinner and thinner. At last, the Red Cross was called in. They built a hospital of ice blocks in the Littlest Snowman's yard — and day and night he was tended by doctors and nurses.

On the day before Christmas, the Littlest Snowman had grown terribly thin. However, just when it was thought that he would melt completely, a howling cold wind came into town from the North Pole. The red Snake in the thermometer dropped with a hiss.

Now the Littlest Snowman went forth to wish his fellow Snowpeople a happy holiday. He wobbled up and down the streets on his thin little snow feet, but nowhere could he find a single Snowperson. They had all melted. The only person he could find was Mr. Weather Man, who was crying great tears.

"It isn't going to snow!" sobbed the Weather Man. "Not a single flake! Oh, people will never forgive me — especially the children!"

"That's not so," said the Littlest Snowman. "Tomorrow is Christmas, and it is always a kind, generous, loving time! Besides, I have an idea for making it snow, so come along with me."

They walked across the park to an ice cream and ices factory. There they bought every last gallon of flavored ices in sight, and had it delivered to the foot of the Biggest Christmas Tree.

"Now," said the Littlest Snowman to the Weather Man, "just watch me!"

First he ate a gallon of strawberry ice, then a gallon of pistachio ice, and then the orange, lemon, lime and chocolate flavors, too. With every gallon he ate, the Littlest Snowman grew fatter — and fatter — and FATTER! At last he had enough and

climbed to the very top of the Biggest Christmas Tree, looking as fat and colorful as a cloud at sunset. Up there, high above the town, the North Wind was so strong that the Biggest Christmas Tree bent and swayed.

"Come down!" shouted the Weather Man. "You must climb down or you'll be blown to pieces!"

"Of course I will!" cried the Littlest Snowman. "And just think of the beautiful snow all the children will have for Christmas!"

Even as he spoke, the fierce North Wind began to pluck the Littlest Snowman as though he were a Christmas goose or turkey. Flakes of every flavor and color flew all over, giving the town the most beautiful Christmas Eve it had ever seen.

But — on Christmas Day — there was no Littlest Snowman at all.

Oh, but the townspeople could not have that! They hunted through the drifts gathering every white flake, and brought them back to the little boy on Winter Avenue. He went to work and in no time at all, there was the Littlest Snowman again as good as new. In fact, he was better than new, because the little boy had added four gallons of vanilla ice to fatten him up.

And when the candy heart was discovered to be still on top of the Biggest Christmas Tree, the townspeople lifted the Littlest Snowman up through the branches and put his heart back in place right there. All Christmas Day and all Christmas Week, the Littlest Snowman sat there with a jolly smile on his happy face. His candy heart beat "I Love You Truly" so loudly that it could be heard in every corner of town. And, after all, as everyone said, "Isn't 'I Love You Truly' just another way of saying 'Merry Christmas'?"